BE LOVE FLOW

into your

PEACE POWER PRESENCE

Published by Seacoast Press, an imprint of MindStir Media, LLC
1931 Woodbury Ave. #182 | Portsmouth, New Hampshire 03801 | USA
1.800.767.0531 | www.seacoastpress.com

Printed in the United States of America
ISBN-13: 978-1-7365224-2-4

BE LOVE FLOW

into your

PEACE POWER PRESENCE

Activations, tools and practices to heal, clear energetic patterns and embody your highest frequency.

KENDRA AMOS

DEDICATION

This book is dedicated to my grandma Gloria whom I will forever admire. To all our late nights and early mornings when I was hustling in New York City for ten years. I miss you in this reality, but I feel you with me all the time, and thank you for visiting me in my dreams when I was at my lowest points.

For my dad, Keni, who has been the most amazing dad in the world to me. You taught me to contemplate life for myself and to stand up to toxic bullies.

For my mom Eva who gave me so much love and told me that I could do anything and be anything, I'm grateful, and I believed you!

To my brother Evan who could karate kick me into a giant Lego tower and then always have my back at the end of the day, even if you aren't the speed of light, I will always love you.

To Winnie, I love you, my twin, and Frenchcore unicorn. You are everything magical.

To Matt thanks for being there for me, you're amazing.

To Michael, I love you. You have been the only partner ever to support me and give me the courage to show up and be all in it to win it. You are my everything.

To the magic mushrooms and trips along the way, and to trance music, you evoke a beautiful storm inside me.

What does it mean
TO BE LOVE FLOW
into your
PEACE POWER PRESENCE?

BE - To be your authentic self, which is love.

LOVE - To embody love.

FLOW - To align with the universe.

PEACE - To feel calm and to have a clear channel.

POWER - To know that you are in control of you and your experience, your energy, and your sacred vessel.

PRESENCE- To be fully present, which is to be at your highest and most powerful frequency.

This book is a program to un-program. I, me, you, we, we are here because we are ready to consciously take control of our reality by embodying our highest frequency. You are ready to re-program yourself instead of continuing to allow yourself to be programmed and continue to run these old programs and stories that are causing inner chaos within your mind, heart, and body. Disconnection comes from being unconscious and confused. Clarity comes from running toward you in every view. Who would you be if you were free? Have you ever asked yourself this question? Who would you be if you were free? The more you become free, the more you see what is possible for you.

Free from disempowering beliefs, patterns, trauma, and past pain. Free from running from yourself. Free from trying to be busy, do more, and force yourself to feel worthy. It's time to stop running from your emotions and no longer be confused about who you are and why you're here.

YOUR FOUNDATION IS CORRUPTED, SO IT'S NOW BEING INTERRUPTED.

We can't just think our way to a better reality. If it were that simple, we would do just that. We must do the inner work of dismantling our beliefs, healing trauma, and understanding and utilizing the right tools for shifting and managing our energy. You can't fake a frequency.

Understanding the dynamic between your thoughts and patterns, which create emotions, which create your energetic vibrational frequency, which manifest your reality, is how you begin to move into a more powerful state, a new you, who is true, in the view.

In this powerful and life-changing book, you will begin to dismantle and rebuild your foundation. Become aware of and understand your past pain and patterns. Begin to heal, balance, and flow through creating sacred space while understanding yourself more. Seeing and feeling where you have been and where you want to go.

Sacred space is when your life becomes a moving meditation. It's an honoring of your truth as you embody the pure love and awareness that you are. It's raising your frequency and being at home within your essence. It's about self-love, boundaries, focusing energy, and setting intentions. Are you ready to drop the stories and let go of the limiting patterns as you give yourself permission to receive unlimited abundance and love through alignment of your truth and your power?

I hear you! It was a fuck yes for me too. While the journey never ends, we must acknowledge what we want, and we must choose ourselves and give ourselves permission to decide consciously. Once we decide, no one and nothing can stop us because that's how powerful we are.

You are powerful. We are powerful. Are you ready?

Chapter 1

ALL THINGS IN THE UNIVERSE ARE MENTAL AND ENERGETIC

"THE ALL IS MIND; The Universe is Mental."--*The Kybalion.*

Your journey will break you, make you, and take you away in every way. Do not fear your rebirth, for you are magic. Give yourself permission to embark on this journey consciously. You're being reborn from form and function to magic and magnificence.

YOU ARE DIVINE... AND YES, YOU ARE TUMBLING DOWN THE RABBIT HOLE.

It's quite beautiful, the sum of your parts and hearts that illuminate and darken your existence, and oh, I know, so much resistance. An insanely chaotic thing, but we are still so much magic. Are we stuck in the labyrinth going round and round, hoping to be found?

FOR THE LONGEST TIME, I WANTED TO DIE.

My parents told me that I was the most grown-up little girl they ever saw, and inside, I felt it too. I felt the weight of the world, the weight of other people's stuff, the weight of my own projections, pain, traumatic experiences, and just in general, I have always felt things very deeply.

Do you feel deeply too? I would sit alone in my room at night and just think and feel and most often cry. In the duality of our experience, feeling deeply and being sensitive is a gift and a curse until you learn how to move energy and become so acutely aware that you know when to protect your energetic space, how to love and how to take care of yourself. Many of us came here in this lifetime to do something, we have a purpose, and it involves getting our shit together so we can help as many people as we can. If you're reading this, it is most likely you are being guided to embody your highest frequency and take action. I want to help you, and I want to tell you everything I know that has guided me to this very moment.

My struggle with being in this reality that did not feel like home to me started early on as a child. I didn't want to be seen, so I did the in-between. Walking between worlds. Somewhere magic and mysterious, I was oh-so-serious trying to figure it all out.

One day I caught my eyes in the mirror, and I didn't look away, but my gaze lingered to stay. And I had to say to myself, "Wow, look at you and this view. Just keep being true. You'll be born anew. You're here. You're doing it. Falling down, looking around, some days, you're lost in the frost and frozen, and some days you're found." Somewhere out there, I started to see and be, and when I faced my inner dark and deep, I realized I was no longer asleep. I saw my mind as a liar, so I set it on fire and embraced my true desire.

When we really feel into the questions, and we start to question it all, we will inevitably fall. The pain is most often the program. Fear. Anxiety. The hiding. The being watered down. Clinging to lost and not yet found, it's quite profound.

When we decide to abide or hide no longer, we end the program. Our power will always lie in our choices. I choose empowerment. What will you choose? What programs are you running? Who would you be if you were free to see and be who you are truly? Will you choose empowerment?

The real you is the silent witness who is powerful and peaceful, love and above. The real you is the presence under the noise within the void. The darkness smashes into your light that you fight. The real you allows full surrender because you remember. Transcend everything until you reach your still point in the night. You are brilliant and bright, so much light, I promise it will be alright.

Welcome, you divine and beautiful soul. I am grateful you are choosing you. From this moment on, things will never be the same for you, and I mean that in a good way.

I've spent so many years going round and round, hoping to be found. We traverse much of the same darkness over our lives, and we struggle. This struggle leads to anxiety, depression, and sometimes suicidal thoughts or even suicide. I know you know this struggle, and I know that's why you are here. You are ready to release your fear and let your power be here. Struggle is part of the journey until we realize how much of our struggle is our choice. This book is filled with downloads and insights I received from many different altered states of consciousness.

I wrote this book to help every soul that I can. My why lies in my experience and knowledge to share and to empower as many souls on their journey as I can. This is my purpose and my mission. I realized that every single experience we experience and every pattern, coding, activation, transformation, healing, and expansion you will face and use the power of your grace to overcome is mental and energetic. Any program, class, or help you may want to utilize, if it does not address the energetic aspect of your experience, you will not be able to make a long-lasting change or transformation. My methodology that I live and that I find success in with my clients always addresses the mental and energetic components because our experience is both mental and energetic.

In this book, there are practices to help you traverse anything you will ever encounter and energy tools to help you find, accept, and embody your own truths and power, so you no longer cower. From my heart to yours, I hope these messages resonate and help you tremendously on your path to embodying more peace, power, and presence. It's always been you that you've been looking for. You are the lock and the key, I hope you see. I hope you have the courage to run toward you in every view and become more true.

ARE YOU READY?

Spirit in flow, you are music and magic in movement.

Are you ready to align with your authenticity? To be unabashedly you, without restraint, always moving in sync with your inner rhythm aligned with spirit in flow. Are you ready to tell fear to fuck off?

You are a divine and beautiful soul. Are you ready to step into your presence and live from a place of peace and power in love with yourself and your experience? When we live from a place of peace and power, we have presence, and we can be love flow. You are powerful. Do you feel powerful?

When you remember that you are powerful and you maintain a peaceful presence inside your sacred space most of the time, then you will know. I know you know you are so ready to be love flow, into your peace power presence. Already finding your flow, down the rabbit hole we go.

HOW THIS BOOK CAME TO BE.

Our journeys are always so crazy, but isn't it interesting how creative musings are born? So many stops and starts, so much resistance and so much growth over the years that I have been writing this. So many insanely low moments and high in the cloud moments. Fear made me burn, then freedom took its turn, and I would learn more and more about what I was choosing.

This book seemingly started with small bits of writing each day. I had no idea what the topic would even be, but I trusted that it would appear if I held space for it to show up. I wasn't even sure from day to day what I would write. I was absolutely terrified that I would run out of things to say and that I would even be able to step back and be objective in my experience as I was up close and living it. As I was writing this book, I kept thinking back to how I once won a writing award in the fourth grade for the first piece I ever wrote. I thought maybe it was just luck. I hadn't written much more than that, but I felt my voice wanting to get out day by day. It started as a whisper, but then it was a roar, so I kept writing more. I made a promise that day by day, I would write small bits and bobs, and I just figured that if I wrote about my experience in all honesty that it might help and inspire others to seek and speak their truth from their hearts. Do you find yourself speaking your heart often from a place of power, passion, and purpose?

In the beginning, it was hard to show up in each moment. Lucky for me, I had a lot of healing to do, a whole hell of a lot to say, a lot of challenging moments that would break me and make me and take me down a new path to become more of me and so you see, this book is just that. Moments of love. The high and the low of the flow, where I drowned so deep, I awoke from more sleep. Moments of such intense lows and past pain that I was terrified of my emotions as they raged on demanding to be seen, felt, and heard as I pulled away from the herd.

What I have realized in writing this book is that in healing ourselves, speaking our truths, being aware, and in honoring our light and dark, we can understand how to be present day by day with all that we are and all that we feel. To begin to expand our consciousness moment by moment. To be able to accept and be with our darkness and our light and to find harmony in how we exist in our day-to-day experiences. That the way to finding our balance is in remembering how to love ourselves and to fall in love with our experiences whatever they may be, and appreciate what every soul we meet teaches us each day.

What I began to realize as I started writing and in the telling of my story is that power is when you make yourself at home in your darkness. Power is when you stop checking out and stop running from your thoughts and emotions. No one can skip the struggle. We can't walk around it or ignore it. There are a season and a reason for every single thing that has brought you to this exact moment.

The most powerful thing I have ever learned is that power is running toward you in every view. Embodying our highest frequency is accepting and acknowledging ourselves in every moment no matter what. No more abandoning ourselves because this is how we get abused by others. When we don't have a practice of connecting with ourselves and a feeling of self-love, we broadcast that to the world and allow others to treat us in an abusive way simply because we abuse ourselves. All is but a mirror for us. When we take the beginning steps to heal and to embody that which is love in balance, we find ourselves becoming inspired to create and to grow. As I worked on consciously healing myself, finding my balance, I began to feel inspired, and I wanted to inspire other souls. I hope that this book inspires you to show up powerfully for yourself.

YOU ARE DIVINE. YOU ARE TUMBLING DOWN THE RABBIT HOLE

No one is given a manual. The only thing we have is our intuition and our connection to spirit and other souls that we meet along the way that bring us messages. These souls inspire us to see and feel the truth of what we need to do next. Everyone experiences trauma, from physical pain and abuse to emotional and mental trauma, and everyone processes it differently. No one is getting out of here alive, but we can do our best to heal ourselves, find balance, and begin to help others. Healing is heavy, and then it's light as things lift away. So often, we can be weighed down by our experiences just as we are lifted and shifted by them.

I believe that as we heal, we feel lighter, love, and awareness as we start to become at home in our darkness. We begin to integrate more dominance and darkness. We understand the importance of claiming all of our pieces. Healing is about isolating, stopping, and staring. It's about looking within. Have you called out your warrior spirit and walked slowly through it all? Stop and stare, and it will meet you there. Do you look away mostly, or do you stay? It's the questions that drive us. It's a whisper then a roar, and you know we want more.

WE ARE ALL BEING INITIATED, MY INITIATION BEGAN EARLY ON, AND MAYBE YOURS DID TOO, THIS IS MY BEGINNING, MY STORY AND MY WHY, FOR THE LONGEST TIME I WANTED TO DIE.

As I mentioned earlier, I spent most of my life not wanting to be here. So confused about why I felt so sad, emotionally chaotic, and drained on a regular basis, I spent most of my childhood depressed, anxious, and suicidal. I never felt as if anyone understood me or could see me, and I couldn't see myself, so self- love evaded me. Not realizing that I was an empath made my path incredibly confusing and challenging. Lost and acting from a place of fear and resistance to my experience, I was plunged into darkness over and over.

After almost two decades of consistent seeking, meditation, and inner work, I learned to thrive and was reborn over and over out of that very darkness. I have come to love my darkness. It was the darkness that transformed me the most. I have come close to dying a few times when cancer arrived at my door at eighteen. I've survived five car crashes, four of them in one year when I came back home to LA. I overcame and came home to myself despite childhood sexual trauma and being raped in college. My dog and I even survived a dog attack together. Metaphorically I have died thousands of deaths. After I got cancer at eighteen, I beat it that same year, eight months later, through chemo and creative visualization, and I quickly realized that everything happens for us, not to us.

Take that in and think about that statement because that means that you are being blessed by any darkness that surrounds you now. It means that everything is happening for you and not to you, and it's your decision to embrace it, face it, and transform yourself. The difference between having a victim mindset and believing that things just happen is disempowerment, and it bleeds into and corrupts everything in your experience and narrative. Believing that everything is happening for you is how you begin to walk home to yourself. It's the first step for taking responsibility for your life and experience.

New things are always born out of chaos, and vulnerability gives us power, so know that you are not weak if you currently feel weak and consumed by your darkness, emotions, and the state of the world. If you feel that you are struggling right now, know that you are being blessed. Initiated. You are getting your chance for empowerment and coming home to you. We can speak our truths, and we can be free. We can choose not to be broken under guilt and shame and suffocated by our baggage to the point where we cannot take flight. We can choose not to be limited or defined by our life experiences. We can write new narratives and choose to expand in love. We can choose to integrate our shadow side and become whole. We all have healing to do as we find our balance. Where we find our balance is where we find our way.

Healing is a miraculous thing, but it always takes time and requires inner work. It requires tools to break out of the programming and patterns we cling to. When we heal ourselves, we are able to make better decisions and maintain our balance, which makes us powerful manifestors. We will be broken many times in our lives, but we will be reborn over and over from form and function to magic and magnificence. We experience the most growth from healing and expanding in love, and it always takes longer than we think it will to heal. The more we resist, the longer it persists.

Through my life experiences and in offering my stories and my truths from my point of reality, I offer my words, support, and love in hopes of inspiring you to claim your truths and step into your full authenticity and full power. Our sexual energy is our power, our voice, our creativity, our healing, and our rebirth. Join me as you claim all of who you are to step fully into your power and full presence, which is your birthright.

Honestly

I have to be honest, I've been afraid most of my life, like most of us are, to speak my truth, to stand out from the crowd, to trust that what I have to say is good enough, and to be authentically me. In the past, I have even been afraid to take chances to stand in my power and step into my authenticity, to deviate from who I am and instead be who they told me to be. More importantly, to find the courage to speak my truth and to stand in my power. Although perhaps from the outside looking in, you would have never guessed it. Fear drove many of my decisions. If only I could achieve more, be prettier, be skinnier, be faster, be stronger, become smarter, and be better, just better in all ways.

The real me, under the mask, the me I truly am, couldn't possibly be enough just as I am right here and right now. The type-A, driven, always-busy-so-I-don't-have-to-face-my-fears, perfectionist me, who was always constantly doing, doing, doing, and pushing things to happen for me. The full-force, masculine-energy, yang-girl me. Now, these are just labels, and labels are limiting, and these are just things, things I thought were the way to do all the things. You understand what I'm saying.

Maybe you are tired of living like this because I know I was. I couldn't help feeling that there was an easier, more fluid way to get things done and to be in balance. Back in the day, I didn't even know what balance was, but I am telling you this because I know you may be feeling the same way right now, and I want you to know that I see you and that I am sending you so much love from my heart to yours. You should know that you are beautiful, just as you are, right here, right now. You are enough and have always been enough. You are so worthy of all the things you want, of all the magical moments you deserve. What I realized, and you should too, is that it is never too late to embrace a new truth—to embrace your truth and to live that truth, love it, and embody it every day on your journey.

Waking up

When I first started waking up, it was back in 1999. I had recently graduated from school and started my first graphic design job in New York City. It was an amazing opportunity, and I was making good money, and I felt so blessed, lucky, and alive! Life was like an amazing dream at that moment, but very shortly after starting my new position, I wasn't feeling that great.

At the time, it didn't seem like such a big deal. I was nineteen, and what was the most that could be wrong? I had my whole life in front of me, and I was so excited to be alive. My mother and I went to visit a doctor, and when he was about to tell us what was wrong, I didn't notice, but he looked pretty serious. He said, "You've got cancer." My mom and I just looked at each other, both shocked. The silence seemed to last for an eternity before my mom spoke and burst into tears. Neither of us saw this coming. It wasn't even a possibility that could have been in our minds at the time. I mean, I was nineteen, hence the shock.

This was the beginning of my life and career, and everything was going so well. How could I have cancer? Cancer is a very serious disease, and a lot of people don't come back from it. It was a huge roadblock when all I wanted to do was work at an amazing job and live my life. I had just landed an amazing job paying six figures doing design work, which was my passion. I was leading this beautiful life that was right in front of me, blossoming and blooming. I was so focused on making money and partying in New York City and having fun. Just living the high life. I was nineteen!

Back to Sleep

As I started waking up, I started facing some of my fears. When I beat cancer—yes, I beat it that same year—I realized I had become a victim of my own mind. Little did I know this was the beginning of stripping away all that I thought I was and knew, and there was so much more to come. I knew that I always wanted to lead a life where, at the end of each day, I could look in the mirror, look into my eyes, and feel good about the decisions I was making and about the life I was leading. Feel good about the way I treated people. Eventually, lead a life where I could make a difference, to help in some way. I knew I didn't feel ready, but I knew I just needed to put myself out there, and that I didn't want to live with regrets.

After finding out that I could have died and that maybe the little bit of life I had led was almost halted by a disease, I figured and felt that the time I originally thought I had wasn't real. No one knows how long we really have. This jolted me into the present. I knew I had to start taking chances, to say things I felt, to not hold back, to dive in. What was the worst that could happen, I thought. I've always had a fighter mentality. I used to do these karate kicks sometimes when I was younger, and I thought they were so cool, but I am sure anyone looking over in curiosity would have thought how ridiculous I was and burst out laughing. I thought, well, all I have to do is work hard. I should just be me and spread my love, light, and truth and release attachment to how things will happen. Trust in divine timing. It's so funny because this sounds like such a great plan and so easy, right? Um, no. Life is simple in theory but so complicated in the actual practice.

Interestingly, I wonder who I would have become if I had not fought cancer at nineteen. It was like when I meet people that I love, I give all I have, and I am passionate to the core. I don't hold back words or wait because I know and respect that tomorrow is not guaranteed. People sometimes seem taken back by how I am so deeply passionate, but I just put it all out there. That is just me.

Truth is, you've heard it before. We will never feel ready, but despite that feeling, it is always the right time to begin. Right here, right now, we must begin! We must trust ourselves; we must trust spirit; we must trust in divine timing and dive in and begin! When I got sick, that was a wakeup call at nineteen, a serious smack in the face. It was as if I could see and feel the truth about our time here. I don't know that anyone is prepared to be told they have a fatal disease and are going to die because that's not peachy.

Beating cancer woke me up. But, once my fight with cancer was won, I sort of nodded off again, back to sleep for the next thirteen years. I was sort of coherent, but I led a life plugged into and focused on surface stuff that didn't matter much, but nevertheless, it was my life. I felt safe and happy that I was alive. I felt lucky, and I took on newfound gratitude that gave me a different view on life than most others around me at the time had. Most people I knew felt like life was a guarantee, and I knew that even tomorrow wasn't promised to anyone. My dad always told me that all asses are up for grabs and that no one person is any better or worse than anyone. Anything can happen and we are all indeed equal.

So I continued on the same path as I was, focused on surface stuff, making as much money as I could at jobs I hated, driving expensive cars, getting a big expensive house, focusing on the race to get married—you know, all the everyday stuff that we are told to want regardless of whether we genuinely feel it's for us or not. Yeah, that stuff. The stuff that makes you feel lonely at night, the stuff that keeps you up wondering why there is a big hole in your heart and why your soul aches for something more, but you can't put your finger on it, and you feel so disconnected from who you truly are. Some of us want these things, and that's good. Some of us don't. If you're happy, you are aligned. If you aren't, then seek deep within for your truth.

Healing, self-reflection, and emotional intelligence is the real journey.

I know you are ready to heal and see what's real.

What is healing? How does one heal, and why is it so important?

The amount of awareness and the way you surrender to your past pain, trauma, and triggers, as you let them pin you to the ground, as you drown, is directly related to whether or not you are found, or just continue to do the round and round. Healing is the process of making or becoming sound or healthy again.

To be healed means to no longer be driven by past pain. To no longer unconsciously react but consciously act. To no longer attract the same type of partners or experiences because you no longer hold those beliefs or energetic blocks and patterns. To no longer take the same actions. To no longer hold a disempowering narrative. Healing is something that takes time and awareness, and it usually takes way longer than we want it to. Or that could just be me because I am an Aries, and being impatient has been a part of my inner dynamic. You get what I am saying, though? You may think, "I have got this," and then there is still more pain or negative emotions to unpack, and more truth as you spin round that spiral and see greater truths. I think embracing the fun of your experience and loving the questions and diving into the adventures is one way not to take things so seriously.

On the other hand, healing is serious. Things break us and make us. No one is perfect, and everyone has a shadow side. This is why the first few months with a new partner seem so amazing, and then the shadows come out to play, and then it's like, "Buckle up because here we go." This is why we don't experience a tremendous amount of growth in relationships. It's crazy. We can continuously follow the same patterns over and over with different people. Dating, getting close, then being afraid to be attached, and then running and starting over. No one wants to get hurt, but getting hurt is what teaches us a lot about who we are and what we want and what we don't want.

Healing is how we step into our true power and how we begin to live from our souls instead of our minds. The mind is a complex and diverse thing. We can't think our way around here. Healing is going to help you see more clearly and be happier. No one gives us a manual, but there are tools that can help you find your way through the many rabbit holes we wander down.

IT'S ABOUT TO GET REAL

What is perception and awareness? Why your mind is a liar, and you need to set it on fire and use it for your desire.

Do you have fear/ego conversations or higher self/soul conversations?

Our power lies in the questions we ask. It's how we remove our mask. In the silence we face, we can take our place with our true face.

OUR POWER LIES IN THE ONGOING
DIALOGUE, OUR SELF-LOVE AND FEAR.
MY DEAR WHAT CAN YOU HEAR?

Chapter 2

IT'S INEVITABLE YOU CAN HAVE IT ALL, BUT FIRST YOU HAVE TO FALL INTO YOUR DARKNESS AND CONQUER IT ALL

ARE YOU READY TO ACCEPT THE INITIATION AND SURRENDER TO EACH CROSSROADS AS YOU TAKE BACK YOUR POWER THAT HAS BEEN SLOWLY STRIPPED AWAY AND BROUGHT YOU TO WHERE YOU ARE TODAY?

What does it mean to fall? If you want to expand and evolve, you have to let go of everything you thought you were, and everything that is, or has been, holding you back. You have to let go of who you thought you were and where you thought you were going. You have to be willing to open your channel up to your connection with the source.

Do you have lower self fear/ego conversations, or higher self soul conversations? Do you even know the difference? Our power will always lie in the questions we ask. It's how we remove our mask. In the silence we face, we can take our place with our true face. Do you feel worthy? Do you feel loved? Do you feel real? Or do you feel like some watered-down version of who you are, and you can't seem to make it too far? Do you feel as though you can see accurately? What is real and what is an absolute truth. Do you feel balanced and stable as if you can focus and control your energy? Do you feel empowered?

If you think you are not worthy, know this, hear this, and feel this. Your foundation is corrupted, so it must be interrupted. This is your interruption. Thinking you are not worthy is a lie that no longer serves—or deserves—your focus. Be true in your view. Let the new move through.

You are worthy. Believe and let that flow into your darkness. Let yourself be transformed at your core. Believe these lies no more. See the truth of that in which you truly are.

You are so worthy. You are so loved, and you are real. You are safe to be who you are, and it will take you far. Stay wild and true in your view. Stay wild in your ways for all your days, in a love-struck haze, with your powerful gaze, let nothing faze you.

Embrace your feelings and let them transform you. There is nothing wrong with you or your feelings. Embrace who you are and your experience. Do not fear your transformation. Let what you feel transform you. Feel it all.

Your worthiness is not predicated on your experiences. Your worthiness is not predicated on how people treat you or see you. It just isn't so. It is not predicated on other people's behavior, perception, lies, abuse, or bullshit.

So often, we look outside of ourselves for answers to how we should feel and what is acceptable and for validation about who we are and how we are seen. So often, it makes us do the in-between and not want to be seen.

When you finally see, you will begin to be free. Whether you believe you are worthy, you deserve it all, fall, have a ball, embrace it all, you are not small.

Have you ever even questioned why you don't feel good about yourself? Where did those feelings even come from? Was it the first time someone made fun of you? Was it the first time you failed? When was it? Did you even ever feel that way as a baby or a young child? Did these feelings only begin to come up when you began to interact with others? When you stepped into society?

Everyone is indoctrinated. Indoctrination: The process of teaching a person or group to accept a set of beliefs uncritically. As we step into society, we are indoctrinated, and we just accept so many things that simply aren't true and things that certainly do not empower us. We use the belief we have been told to build the foundation of our life, and we then live according to this, and these very beliefs shape our reality.

We all have a higher self and a lower self. Your higher self is a term associated with multiple belief systems, but its basic premise describes an eternal, omnipotent, conscious, and intelligent being, who is one's real self. The lower self is the you that is trapped in the illusions, false conclusions, and lies that we build our sense of self upon and construct our ego-personality-identity around.

Who are you in this view? All you have to do is be true. What is true, and what is you? Have you ever simply asked when thinking a thought before believing it, is this true? Is this an absolute truth or a relative one? We are so programmed to the point where it is hard to challenge ourselves and our foundation, everything that has brought us to this moment.

In Hoodoo, a crossroads is any road where two roads cross. It is said that crossroads is a place without time and full of magic. The crossroads is a place of power, and when we find ourselves at a metaphoric crossroads when a decision has to be made, something has to be overcome, or something big is about to shift, we are in a moment where we are about to exchange one version of who we are for the next.

There are many crossroads we come to as we travel many roads in our lifetime, decisions that need to be made. We can certainly resist and take the long way round, and in fact, I feel as though we do quite often resist trusting in our experience. We resist trusting in ourselves. I started to see that I, me, you, we, we can have it all. But it's true, first, we have to fall into our darkness. See our bullshit that I, me, you, we have been letting hold us back. We have the power to be and do anything, but we are the only ones holding us back. Tick tock, we are the lock and the key, and I hope you can start to see, you can decide to be free. We can decide to be better.

What are the crossroads you have come to in your life? What have you had to endure, cross, and survive?

I want to share some of my major crossroads moments with you, and I want you to think about what yours have been. As you think about them, I want you to remove any shame you feel about what you think you should have done differently because these feelings are still holding you back. I want you to feel proud for surviving whatever the outcome as it has brought you to this very moment. I want you to expand and tell a new story about how you did the best you could with the knowledge you had on the frequency you were living in at the time. Honor the level of consciousness you were at and how you were existing then. I want you to begin to forgive yourself and other people you feel wronged you. I want you to fully embrace and integrate your experiences in an empowering and positive way to build you up.

MY FIRST CROSSROADS - 1979 - I, me, you, we, we must remember, remember our reason, and we will rise through every season.

Our first initiation and crossroads, I believe, begins when we are born on this planet. The quest for understanding who we are and why we are here is the biggest crossroads we cross as we discover time and again more of who we are as we have to make decisions that will take us down one path or the other. As we decide, we either move closer to who we are or further away. We either show up, or we hide. We are asked time and again who we really are and why are we here, and how are we going to interact with others? What are our intentions, and what do we want, and how will we show up in a powerful way to be able to receive the life we truly want? The past forty-one years of my life, in this lifetime, has been the biggest challenge. Are you feeling this challenge as you become more conscious and show up more and more? Where are you right now in your life? How are you feeling, and where are you going? What are you still wondering about yourself?

MY SECOND CROSSROADS - I, me, you, we, we are forever bright, and no one can truly dim our light. Every trauma is a call to rise and no longer compromise who we are. We are god. We are divinely protected and never neglected or misdirected. I used to feel so much shame about being sexually abused as a child. I used to feel so drained by toxic people. I was afraid to show up in a powerful way as I truly am. I was afraid of being attacked, so I hid. Understanding energy tools protects you from many negative things because you learn to trust your intuition and gut feelings about certain situations and people. You learn how to self-regulate and calm your storms, especially if you find yourself in a toxic situation or encounter a toxic person. There will always be challenges, but no one can possess or steal that in which you are. Your essence is yours. Have you realized that every single thing that happens is simply a catalyst for change as you exchange versions of who you thought you were for who you actually are?

MY THIRD CROSSROADS - When I was raped - I, me, you, we, many have been raped, and it silenced our voice, but we must choose to heal and deal with what happened.

I remember thinking over and over that I didn't get held down or hit or beaten, and I kept rationalizing that it wasn't that bad. My mind was trying to tell my heart a different truth. If it wasn't that bad, why did I feel worthless? Why did I feel so stupid? Why did I want to jump the fuck out of my body? Why? Why? Why? I said no over and over, but then it happened so fast. He forced himself on me, and in that moment, I felt so confused because it wasn't my decision, and I never once said yes. I didn't want it, and the violation destroyed me in that moment and over time. It eroded my self-esteem. I didn't feel safe in my body or experience for a long time, and I had no idea how to heal or how to release that trauma from my body. How was I going to be okay? This beautiful body I'm in, how can I enjoy pleasure when my experience with sex was disgusting? I was not held in high regard and respected.

It took me twenty-one years from that year to be able to enjoy sex and to feel safe. It took mirror work. It took a tantra self-pleasure practice. It took a lot to come home to me. There are still moments when I am going through hard times, I struggle to allow and receive pleasure, but at least now I am aware and can shift and move that energy through ritual and practice. It took me a long time to heal from the sexual abuse I experienced as a child and that rape in college. It took a lot for me to be able to express what I want and to be present instead of dissociating and leaving my body during intense sexual moments. Often in life, people do things to us, and we are left to deal with the mess. Almost everyone I know has been through something like this. If you have been, how are you healing? How are you rewriting this story as you heal to feel empowered? How are you calling your power back?

MY FOURTH CROSSROADS - Beating cancer - 1999 - I, me, you, we, are not the sum of our parts, but we are our hearts as we expand into our power and no longer cower to the things that happened to us, but we realize it was all for us.

When I got cancer back in 1999, I knew I wanted to do something special with my life, something that deviates from the traditional day to day of just working any job and just getting by. At the time, I had no idea what that would be. Fast forward, March of 2015, I launched a recruiting business to help creative talent find new opportunities. After four years of working for a big agency, I knew it was time to do my own thing, but I didn't feel quite ready. At this point, it was just an idea that came drifting in and out, here and there, but launching a company can be a bit scary. So I took a job in Brooklyn at another agency because I wanted a false sense of safety, and I thought I had it. I thought I was safe playing small and doing the work I had always done, but I kept feeling drawn to do my own thing, and I had a feeling that the universe thought it was time for me to move on as well.

Shortly after getting that feeling through my intuition, I was fired. I remember going home and feeling like I had no worth. I remember

feeling a sense of relief and being lost and scared. I remember thinking, well, what now? I was such a type-A, work, work, work type of
person. I used my job to identify my sense of self and self-worth. The
majority of my self-worth was predicated on my job, and my false
identity I showed to the world was what I was achieving and what I
had acquired, my wealth. I was filled with thoughts of not knowing
how I would spend my days and feeling like I didn't have much of an
identity.

After a few days had passed, something happened. I felt a little
shift. I felt happy, positive, renewed, and ready to start again. I felt
excited that I was driving. I was going to choose exactly what I wanted
to do and how I was going to show up. I felt excited that I didn't have
to show up in a work environment where people treated a professional
environment like it was their personal playground to play games and
instigate drama. I kept thinking, "I know what to do, I know how to
treat me," and without all these people who are out of balance not
doing any inner work without the emotional and energetic drain, I
can begin to achieve what I want. I started getting excited. I felt free.
I was like, let's do this thing. I was not exactly sure how, but ready
to do it!

The inner drive and momentum started to build because now the
space was open for it to arrive, and I started to feel alive! I decided to
start meditating, and I decided to begin working on launching my
new company. Now I was beginning to brim with excitement for the
new thing that was about to be built. I built it, and for a few years, I
did my own thing while partying on yachts in Mexico and traveling
through Europe multiple times a year. I was living the life I wanted,
and I chose me for the first time, and it felt good. People would often
ask, aren't you scared? I was more scared to work for someone who did

not have good intentions for me, who was an emotional mess, someone from whom I never knew what I would get because they were not in their power and unhappy. I did not want any part of that.

As time passed, I knew this wasn't quite the job for me. I wanted to help people heal, but how would I? I still had a lot more to learn before I could help. It would be three years before my entire reality and world would change. Did you ever have to change jobs and create something of your own? When was the last time you felt excited about life and the work you were doing?

MY FIFTH CROSSROADS - An abusive relationship - I, me, you, we can survive, we are more powerful than we will ever know, and in that, we flow.

Around the same time that I had my own business, I was also in an abusive relationship. It was becoming more apparent that it was not going to work. As I was diving deep into my inner work and darkness, I realized more and more about who I was and who he was not. He was drinking all the time to the point of being blackout drunk, and we were drifting apart. We no longer belonged together, and it was time to leave the house, time to leave him and be by myself.

I was meditating by this time every single day because I was not feeling well, and it was getting worse and worse, and I was getting really scared. I felt drained, confused, scared, and far away from me and who I really was. At every turn, he said the things I was interested in were stupid. Meditating and taking a minute for myself and being late to greet our guests was me being selfish. I was being told to ignore me and pretend to be happy.

I remember when we would travel, he let me walk home alone in Europe because drinking and getting drunk were more important than my safety. I remember the day he told me that I shouldn't feel so much. When I told him that if I spent too much time around people, I would feel drained and cry. He didn't understand and suggested that I turn it off. The worst was that from the outside, everything looked great. We had a beautiful house, and we traveled so much, but he was drunk all the time. When he would go blackout, he would say the worst things to me, and then he wouldn't remember how terrible he had been to me and want things to go back to how they were, but it was eroding everything, and I started to feel sick, and it was getting worse. He never took responsibility for anything he did and would spin everything on me.

This was the first time I learned about being gaslit. I started to question myself and wonder, was it that bad, or was I just too sensitive? I began to doubt myself and walk on eggshells. The fighting was daily, and I cried often. I was exhausted. I remember I became dizzy every single day, and they couldn't find out what was wrong with me. It got worse until it was all day every single day. This went on for about a year, 365 days. I pretended it wasn't happening. When I say I pretended, what I am saying is that I didn't want anyone to think I was weak, so I continued to rock climb and run daily. I continued to work and live my life. I saw a nutritionist, I went to the doctors, I changed my diet, I slept more, and nothing helped. I refused to slow down at first, constantly working, wanting, and trying to prove I was worthy and healthy. I had no self-worth based on anything except what I did. I look back now and see how sad this was. How sad I was. I was so fucking sad. How sad and lost I was back then. I had no boundaries and no self-love. I had a high threshold for pain, and it felt familiar to be in this awful situation. This went on for years until I became physically ill.

One night he made me walk home alone so he could continue getting drunk. He was blackout again and told me that he believed I was pretending to be sick and that none of it was real. When he said those words, something in me snapped, broke, I was done. I was no longer kind of mad or sad, I was in a rage, and I felt so disrespected I remember crying in the bathroom and wanting to die. What happened in that relationship put me into a hole that took me years to dig myself out of. Have you had to leave a toxic and abusive partner who couldn't show up for you from a place of love and respect? How do you tell the story now? For me, I take full responsibility that I allowed it to happen, and it was a big lesson in self-love, boundaries, and healing.

During this time in my twenties, I began seeking heavily. Taking every class and reading every book I could find on healing, consciousness, and feeling called to know me and to expand. I knew that I would have years of healing before I could help anyone else, but I kept feeling as though I was going to help people. I just had no idea how yet. I did also know that it would be years of showing up for me before I could show up for anyone else.

MY SIXTH CROSSROADS - A dog attack, a car crash, and a broken heart - All at once in LA- I, me, you, we, are always ready. No matter what it seems or looks like, if it's at your door you're ready for more, and you'll probably hit the floor but conquer ever more. When I came back to LA a few years ago, I had no idea what was about to happen. I grew up in the Valley, and I was so excited to come back home where I knew I belonged.

My resistance to finishing this book when it was mostly done was the worst thing I have ever had to overcome. It wasn't that I have ever had a loss for what to say; it was more that I was living in the illusion and story of not ready yet. It was absolute bullshit, but really, I had energetic blocks about being seen, so even though I was showing up pretty consistently, I was stuck. As soon as we arrived in LA, I was so full of hope and excitement about my life. Within two weeks after we arrived and moved into a new place, everything fell apart.

I was supposed to be working on my book, and my boyfriend at the time was bored, so he suggested we go to the park. My dog, Miles, was so excited we took him. I remember feeling like something was wrong. I felt put off in the weirdest way. The minute we started walking up the street, my boyfriend had the leash, and two big black bull mastiffs crashed into Miles, all fifteen pounds of him, knocking him down. He tumbled over and over. Before I knew it, one of them charged him and started biting him and shaking him. I felt the wind knocked out of me; the voice went out of my body. This attack seemed to go on for an eternity. I heard *He's going to die! Do something!* in my head and so I threw myself on top of Miles. The dog was dragging me. I heard the owner say they just wanted to play, and my blood ran cold as I knew these people were dark and crazy. They had no control over their dogs.

After what seemed like an eternity of getting thrown around and watching my dog get shaken like a rag doll, I stood up, clutching my dog, Miles, to my chest and made it over to the fence to catch my breath. The dog ran over and jumped onto my back and almost knocked us to the ground. It took all my strength to hold onto him and stand strong. I was fucking horrified. I couldn't speak, but a range and rage of emotions were spinning me out. When I finally could look at Miles, the people just walked away as though it was no big deal. Miles was shaking, covered in blood, with bite marks all over his body. His jaw was broken in half, and he had scratch marks all around his eye. He was shaking, and I was shaking in disbelief. A trip to the park turned into this whole other thing.

Seeing the shape Miles was in, I chose to get him to the hospital instead of going after the owners. It cost me five thousand dollars in cash to get his jaw wired back together. After the operation, he was in so much pain that he refused to eat on his own, so we had to spoon-feed him baby food for a while. Every night I slept on the floor with him and gave him Reiki, and he healed incredibly fast even though he was over ten years old at the time of the attack.

The week after that, my boyfriend at the time begged me to buy his brother a plane ticket, and so I did. His brother came to visit and, on the way to take him to the airport, we got hit at high speed while stopped on the freeway. My Audi truck turned off, filled with smoke, and we were stuck in the middle of the highway. After that accident, I was advised to have neck and back surgery and was told I wouldn't be able to run again. It was a few months of not being able to walk or do anything physical. My truck was so messed up that it took over ninety days for them to fix it.

With all of this and after the car crash, I found out that my back may be fractured, and a disc may be out of alignment. At this point, I was sore, mentally, physically, and emotionally drained, quite often on the verge of tears. Simple things like getting out of the car to grab groceries felt like a struggle.

I had days where I knew that nothing was going to get done and that I needed to clear my calendar for the day because I didn't want to leave my apartment, and all I did was cry all day. Then it got worse. Insomnia started. I have always been a good sleeper. I used to sleep sitting up anywhere, but a few days after the accident, now I was faced with nights of waking up every single hour, so now there seemed to be no rest from my mind or the stress of everything that was happening. Then it got even worse. I was crying so much and in a very negative downward spiral. I was all alone except for Miles, who I felt like I had almost let die. I started having sleep paralysis. I started seeing stuff in the corner of my room taunting me, and I kept hearing, "No one can help you." My heart was racing at night while trying to sleep and at random times during the day.

That was very scary, but I stayed calm so that I didn't make it worse. As I write this now that a few years have passed, I want to laugh because I was straight-up not having a good time at all. I couldn't concentrate on anything—writing, working—everything I attempted felt like I was in quicksand and that I couldn't even breathe. Then my hair fell out.

As diverse as we are in our feelings and our strengths and weaknesses, a part of me wanted to crawl into bed and just lay there until I died. I had a few close friends in LA, but I was never one to cry in the corner, so I tried to face all that was happening with the bravest, best face I had. The other part of me kept championing me to keep fighting and not give up. Just breathe and crawl forward until I could run again. This sounds pretty awful, right? I am sure you have been through some crazy hard things in your life, but I know you kept fighting and breathing and moving forward as best as you could if you're reading this. If you are struggling right now, this is your sign that things are going to be okay. I just know it. There were so many days and nights I didn't eat or sleep. I just laid in bed an absolute mess, not knowing what to do.

During this time, I started feeling haunted by the sexual abuse as a child and the rape in college, two things I had not told anyone. I just carried them with me in silence for decades. I decided to tell my parents because I did not want them to read about it but to hear it from me first. I have the best parents; they are incredibly supportive, and they were one hundred percent supportive when I told them all that had happened to me. When I look back, this was the absolute worst and best time of my life.

MY SEVENTH CROSSROADS - In full surrender, I, me, you, we surrender. Psychedelic trips and kriyas and tripping out. We can be a beautiful mess and still show up.

When everything started happening in LA is when I had no more space for any more trauma, and I knew it was time to start finding tools to heal. I was maxed out. I knew I was maxed out because I was sad, I was emotionally unstable, and I was depressed and had anxiety. For the first time in my life, my heart would race while lying down at night. My body was asking me to love myself. It was asking me to be present and to really listen. To stop just moving through life unconsciously. To start taking responsibility for me and my life and how I was showing up, and I wasn't. I was hiding.

I was spending every moment at shows, and yes, I love music, but I was not learning and growing. I was regularly checking out through exercising and partying. The first two years back in LA, I must have done over a hundred shows. Music will always be life to me, but I had no balance at all. I had gotten a large sum of money, but I had no direction, and I wasn't even sure what I wanted to do. I had a year of finding myself. I started to realize I had to start showing up powerfully every day as the beautiful fucking mess and confess. I realized that my stories and my development were here to help people on their paths. This was true because people kept coming to me the next year and asking me to coach them, and I didn't have a formalized methodology yet. I had discovered sound healing, which changed my life, and I already knew Reiki from years before, and when I added in oil alchemy, it all came together.

I want you to think about all the crossroads moments in your life that you have walked through, crawled through, cried through, and whatever regrets you may still have. Please release them. Please take some time to forgive yourself and others. Take some time to tell these stories in a more empowering way that will empower you. Think about and feel into how these moments defined you in some ways and released you in others. The very fabric of your being has evolved, expanded, and grown because of these experiences. I challenge you to see your past and future experiences from different vantage points and be open to rewriting them to empower you.

Chapter 3

ENERGY SHADOW AND LIGHT, YOU'RE FOREVER BRIGHT

Now that you've asked the questions, next comes cutting through the illusions. WHO WOULD YOU BE IF YOU WERE FREE? FREE FROM FEAR AND PAST PAIN. FUCK FEAR. DON'T LET IT STAY NEAR AND WHISPER IN YOUR EAR AND STEER WHAT YOU DO AND HOW YOU CREATE YOUR VIEW. JUST BE AWARE AND SHIFT FROM THERE.

Do you ask yourself the real questions? Our power lies in not only the questions we ask but the decisions we make and the chances we take. It's the questions that drive us. It's a whisper then a roar, and we want more. As we expand, then comes the resistance AND PERSISTENCE. To know who we are and to find and embody our truths, that is our life's mission. The most powerful question you can ask yourself is: have you chosen? Are you ready to choose because you can never lose? Are you ready to choose you in every view and to be true?

I ask you this because this is where your power lives, this is where clarity comes. I spent years hiding, looking away, and not knowing how to stay and play the game of life. Do you look away or stay? We've all done it, hiding and checking out because we struggle to self-regulate and calm our own storms. The feeling that comes before we binge eat or decide to starve ourselves another day. The false sense of control as we crash against our emotions, hoping to make them go away, so we don't have to play. The downing of drugs every day so we can hide away. The hurting of others so we can feel better about who we are. There are so many things we use as defense mechanisms, coping mechanisms so we can just survive, but without the inner work, we can never thrive because we are in a perpetual state of running from ourselves. We run because we empower the projections of our mind because we don't know how to feel safe in our bodies and our experience. Mostly your mind is a liar, so set it on fire and align with your true desire.

Now that you've asked the questions, next comes cutting through the illusions.

What patterns do you use to survive? What patterns do you have mentally and energetically that stop you from being empowered? What patterns hold you back? Do you shut down during disagreements? Do you leave your body often? Do you ever run toward you when you feel uncomfortable? Do you ever do energy work to move things through the view?

What patterns emerge when you self-sabotage? What is your energy saying to the world? Do you feel safe enough to be seen, or are you doing the in-between? Who would you be if you were free? Free from fear and past pain. Free from defense mechanisms. Stop fear, and don't let it stay near. Are you ready to begin to be aware and shift from there?

Our minds are simply a projection. For a long time, we believe we are our thoughts and that the stories we create are real. We believe in the meaning that we assign to things. We believe everything to be real and the only truth. As we expand our consciousness, we begin to see that our minds simply project, and we start letting go, and we use our minds for their purpose when they are needed, not to worry and chase monsters in our head mindlessly, but as tools. The mind is designed to look for problems, so no wonder we chase monsters in our minds.

Everyone we see and everything that happens is put through a lens that is distorted. A distortion of who we think people should be, of what they meant versus what they said. What they did and what that meant, what did it mean? Even reading this as you begin to expand your mind and open yourself up to train yourself to see many vantage points, you will begin to free your energy. Your energy will begin to stay more balanced as you watch and contemplate with openness instead of a close-minded view, and then at some point, you may not even contemplate these things or be bothered by what others are doing. You will begin to realize that everyone is on a journey, and we are all the same. You may even begin to feel exhausted when thinking and traveling the same pathways you used to use. As you create new pathways, you begin to realize that the old thought process and beliefs were downright exhausting, and you no longer care to leak and waste energy.

Patterns - One of the most empowering things is realizing your patterns and how you operate under different circumstances. Everyone has patterns and defense mechanisms that serve us until they serve us no more, and we want to reach a new state of mind, a new vibrational frequency, a new us, or maybe it is the old us that we were before we started using them. All trauma and patterns are stored in our energy fields, in our auras, and they continue until we are made aware of them, and we begin to clear them away and transcend them.

Awareness is key. Energetically you can clear and heal anything with the use of energy tools.

Before I used energy tools and looked at my life, I noticed I had become unavailable and closed off. It didn't help that I had been in a few relationships that didn't go well. That I allowed myself to be treated poorly was no one's fault but my own. We get what we allow and accept. I began to see relationship patterns, which I had to assess closely. I also began to ask what was my energetic field and beliefs were saying to the world about how I wanted to be treated, what I would accept, what I wanted, what I needed? What was my trauma saying to the world?

Do you feel safe to be seen by the world, family, friends, partners? Do you feel safe during intimacy with your partner? Do you feel safe to enjoy your pleasure and be in the moment? One of the consequences of being abused mentally, emotionally, sexually, or physically is not wanting to be seen. I hid for a very long time because I did not feel safe to be seen. This world is crazy and we often don't feel safe. Safety starts as a child with your parents and how your inner world is built. Fortunately, my parents were very caring and helped me build a strong foundation to know that I could do anything or go anywhere. I never had to fight my family. I know many are brought up in toxic environments where they never feel safe ever anywhere. I knew I was safe to be me at home, and my parents encouraged me to be strong. I knew whatever happened, my parents would do anything they could to help me be successful or feel safe, whether that be emotionally or financially, and I am grateful. There is much work to do when we don't feel safe. Inner child work is very powerful, as well as other tools like sensory deprivation.

On my second float, I went into the tank to do some forgiveness exercises for myself and the people who abused me, and I remember I had to do these exercises for years to finally release the really hard things that had happened to me. It doesn't just go away after one time; trauma is incredibly debilitating, and I often would ask myself after a plant medicine trip, is pain real? I asked this because yes, I do believe that pain is real, but every time we replay these stories, and we don't have the tools to heal, we are activating the same awful feelings over and over again, increasing and intensifying them. I remember it was late at night so many nights for years, denying what actually happened to me and then remembering over time. I remember dissociating during intimacy because I was constantly being retriggered and felt unsafe and uncomfortable with partners. Those events and stories were such a big part of me. They lived so deeply in me at that time that I didn't know how to release or how to heal or where to start. One of the worst feelings in the world is feeling hurt, abused, sad, depressed, anxious, and suffocated, and not knowing how to feel better or when the feelings are going to overtake you. Where will you be? How long do you have to endure these feelings?

Partway through my journey, as I continued to fight and traverse my darkness and the deep feelings that overtook me, often at any moment, I kept wondering who am I really? Who would I be if I were free? Free from these things, this energy, these stories. How do they help me, what can I learn, how can I help others? I had so many questions. I got so sick of feeling stuck and feeling so heavy and lost. It felt as though it was always going to be with me, and I was always going to feel that way.

Fast forward, at age forty-one in this lifetime after two decades of reading and classes and silence and meditation and asking and watching and learning and going down rabbit hole after rabbit hole, I came to these realizations about how to heal and how to move forward with hope in my heart, a present mind and an awareness that helps me be and see without reacting to internal and external things constantly. Who would you be if you were free? What things do you still need to heal? There are many tools to help heal from trauma. The most powerful are energy tools, but once you are aware and on your journey, you will know in your heart what is right for you and what to do next. Please trust yourself.

Also, know that the strongest and oldest souls sign up for the hardest things because we are here to help others. We are here to make this world a better place and be a light in the dark for others who still cannot see the light and are in the fight every night. Please take some time to think about this chapter. Ridding yourself of limiting patterns is a powerful thing. Ask yourself what experiences keep repeating and what you would like to manifest.

Chapter 4

ENVISION AND EMBODY YOUR HIGHEST FREQUENCY. COME HOME TO YOUR ESSENCE

Do you feel peaceful? Where does your vibrational frequency live?

Do you feel peaceful? How often do you feel peaceful? Is feeling peaceful important to you?

Sometimes we have interactions that result in either another soul or us losing their temper and reacting instead of acting from a conscious and powerful place. Much of what is happening in the world as far as conflict is because of people being completely out of balance and disconnected from source, themselves, and other people. Better balance and feeling joyful begins with our vibrational frequency. Vibes are everything.

Whether or not we feel good has a lot to do with our thoughts and beliefs. We have to ask ourselves what some of our beliefs, truths, and general thoughts are modeled after. We also have to consider if what we feel emotional about is a real thing that needs attention or something that our fear has created to keep us distracted and in a lower vibration. For instance, if we go through a break-up or someone close to us passes away, these are genuine losses and things we need to process, as opposed to believing in some external rule that we believe will validate us, such as, if I was a size four, I would be happy. Or if I looked this way or had that. Negative thinking keeps us on a low vibration. We have to carefully ask ourselves if what we are buying into is a relative truth or an absolute truth. So many things are subjective, like the color of something or what happened. Everything we believe is shaped through a lens of our beliefs, our fears, and our past pains. Sometimes it is quite hard to know what that is. The more we awaken and grow, the more we have a responsibility to objectively ask what we truly know and what about what we know can we strip away and be more open and fluid about. Ultimately whatever beliefs no longer lift and support us on our growth need to be bent, broken, burned, and banished.

So when we have emotions such as fear, shame, guilt, anger, and pride, our vibrational frequency is living between 20 to 175. Courage is at 200. Neutrality is 250, and acceptance is at 350, and that is when we begin to expand. So from 350 and below, we are in a contracted state. It is said that most of the vibrational frequency of the planet lives at 207, which is pretty low considering love or above starts at 500. It appears that at 350, which is acceptance, we begin to expand. 540 is joy, 600 is peace, 700+ is enlightenment. As we raise our vibrational frequency, we raise the frequency of the planet. This is why it is so important that we do the inner work to resolve past pain and contemplate and direct what we believe and what we think.

I have done much contemplation over the past two decades, and I know that the inner negative voice that we hear is a result of brainwashing and lies about who we are and why we are here. As we go within and do battle through all the pieces of light and dark, we can turn the negative voice down or have the awareness to power pause to decide how we are going to act or what we are going to listen to. Most people's minds are loud because they aren't meditating, and they are getting pulled in circles, nor do they know how to accept what they are feeling, call it in, accept it, transmute it, withdraw the energy and bring something positive into its place. That is a really powerful practice.

Over time my inner negative voice has changed because I have consciously chosen to create new neural pathways to travel over, more positive ones that support my happiness and my growth. I have built new truths in my mind, so I have created a new reality from my new perceptions. I have to be honest though, I don't know that the negative voice will ever go away completely, and if it doesn't go away, then we have to think about how we are going to proceed.

Are we going to live under the wave of confusion and be smashed and suffocated, or are we going to fight back and get a fucking surfboard? Are you going to surf? I have become good at surfing, and I want to surf. Will you join me? Get a surfboard and know that you can stay in flow. Accept whatever you are feeling and withdraw the energy. Choose to bring in a higher, better thought and surf the shit out of that. I don't want to live under the wave of confusion, and I know you don't want to either for your whole life. There is such a beautiful sea to see, and we can surf all over. So choose to bring your power to the front and push your fear to the back. You are in control, step into your full power and decide right here, right now what you want. Get your surfboard and figure out how you are going to surf over the negative things in your mind and the negative things around you. Create that sacred space and stay on your board!

Where does your frequency live? Are you aware and tuned in when your energy shifts up or down based on your thoughts?

Chapter 5

WHEN YOU'VE BEEN IN THE DARKNESS LONG ENOUGH YOU BEGIN TO SEE. ARE YOU ALMOST FREE?

HOW WILL YOU EMBRACE YOUR DARKNESS AND INTEGRATE IT SO YOU CAN BE WHOLE?

Healing requires isolation. With isolation comes the awareness to choose. How often do you honor what you need and choose you?

You are, and embody, shadow and light. Everything will be alright. Our darkness is the patterns and pain and the shame we carry that drives us insane and causes us to be split. Split energy is wasteful. We have access to so much energy each day. It is very limited based on the commitments we have. If you use energy tools regularly, then you understand how to conserve, manage, clear, and ground to harness more energy. If you understand alignment, then you know how to conserve and focus energy and not waste it on the mindless disempowering stories in your mind that have created your foundation for a very long time.

Heal yourself

As it began for me

As a child growing up, I was quite depressed and felt so much it seemed compared to other kids my age. I couldn't tell the difference between my energy and the energy of others. At the time, I didn't know that I was highly empathic and struggling, holding on to others' energy that was not mine. I also had my own issues I needed to heal, more on that later. I also grew up being a mixed child in the seventies in a small town, where I always felt out of place. My big curls had their own zip code. By the time I reached my teenage years, my breasts had their own zip code too. So here I was, wanting to hide, but that wasn't possible anymore. I was always getting made fun of and never feeling like I fit in, being told that I was ugly and called "wild woman," which is actually kind of funny now, but most of us have these types of stories from our childhood.

Just when I thought the depression had somewhat passed, and I was in high school starting to feel a little like my own person, my parents were getting a divorce, and my world seemed as though it would be torn apart again, but I survived the rocking of the ship. When my parents finally got divorced, I felt even more alone and isolated. It is never fun when you have to choose between two parents that you love. I remember feeling incredibly suicidal when my parents got divorced. I remember being very close many times to ending it. It is a gift, and a curse to feel incredibly deeply and not know how to process and move through the chaotic thoughts, the high and low energy as a child. Growing up, life just felt hard. Hard as hell and confusing. Yes, there were magic moments, but mostly, I felt so lost, I felt so sensitive, I felt so emotional, and I took everything personal to the point of letting things destroy me. Mostly I was popular, but then I also got bullied sometimes. I just kept thinking, "Damn! Life is a fucking shit show. Like, what the hell?" Because we all know, there is no manual when we are born. It's like, "Good luck, you! Figure it out on your own." Insert crying laughing emoji.

Finally, college came, and I was off to art school. My parents raised me to be grateful for all that I had and to be kind to everyone. They also told me to think for myself and that my brother and I could do anything and go anywhere. I have to thank my parents as they gave my brother and me a strong foundation to go out into the crazy Wild West of the world armed with confidence in what we could achieve in the world.

As I headed off to college, I was fresh-faced, full of excitement, hope, and love. College was a time of finally feeling a bit more at home within myself. Looking back now at how I felt at twenty-seven versus thirty-eight, I wasn't even close to coming home to myself, but I was moving closer. The mind's narratives are a funny thing. How we perceive things is funny, as well.

At art school, I felt alive. Expressing myself through creativity, I was at home drawing, creating, and doing what I loved. I was so excited about life. I just felt so lucky all the time. I loved painting class and graphic design. I felt like I was floating on clouds. Finally, I graduated. I was officially a recent graduate of art school, so full of life, young, naïve, not yet crushed under the wheel of life as I saw it. When I would see people sad and upset or struggling, I couldn't fully understand because I felt so full of hope, happiness, and excitement to be alive!

I felt those things, but having beaten cancer brought in gratitude, and it brightened everything. It was like I was lit and high on life to a level that most people weren't because they had never been threatened with losing it all. Most of my childhood, I felt depressed and out of place, but somehow it began to lift finally, and I felt lighter. My dad would always say in his wise fatherly voice, "You don't know much yet," although I begged to differ at the time. I couldn't quite fathom how far I would travel physically, mentally, emotionally, and spiritually, not realizing how little I did know.

Even as I think about the fact that I have been seeking at this point for years and years finally claiming my truths, I still know nothing except one thing, and that thing is that love is real. In thirty-eight years, the only thing I know without a doubt is that love and connection are real, and that's it. So you may want to throw this book in the trash or get your money back. Just kidding. There may be a few things I have picked up along the way.

So I had just moved to New York City and gotten an amazing job as a graphic designer. I felt that life was limitless, and I could go anywhere and do anything. I felt on top of the world! I landed a job doing what I loved with a six-figure salary. I couldn't believe how lucky I was. It was a magical time. For a moment.

Within the first month, I didn't feel so great, which was strange because I was healthy, I thought. I was exhausted, which was strange for a nineteen-year-old who worked out and took good care of herself. Shortly after visiting the doctor, I found out I had cancer, non-Hodgkin's disease. When the doctor told my mom and me, she started crying, but I didn't feel sad or scared. I felt like I could beat this, and I just didn't feel that it was a big scary deal. I was possibly young and naïve, or maybe my trust in the universe was stronger than my fear because I felt like, "I've got this." It felt like when you're worried, and your BFF is like, I got you. I knew I had it. I could beat this, no doubts.

I spent a year working full-time on a night shift while I was sick, while I received my chemo treatments every week after work. My boss begged me to take time off, but I plowed right through it, making it look easy. All I could think was that I was glad I had my dad and mom to support me. Deep down inside, I didn't want anyone to think I was weak, so I took only a few days off. I think I took three days off from work in the eight months I was getting treatment. I know, I am a savage. My dad took me to chemo every week after work my last night shift. I was so grateful we got to spend all that time together. I felt so much love from my friends and family. I felt grateful to be alive, and I wasn't really scared. Losing and death never entered my mind for more than a few seconds. I felt like a warrior, ready to wield my sword and fight till the death, and quite literally, I knew it might come to that.

The year that I was told that I had cancer, eight months later and after rounds of chemo, I was cancer-free. That was twenty-three years ago this month. That time that I was sick, I spent a lot of time with my grandma Gloria, she was my favorite grandma. Such a bright smile, high cheekbones, so sassy and always positive and always spoke her truth even to a fault. She could cook up a storm and seemed to dance when she walked. A famous writer, she was witty and lit up a room when she entered it. She had these long legs, and I imagined how she used to dance at all the parties she attended when she was younger.

Over the years, as my grandma grew older, she also grew sick. In the end, she couldn't speak anymore, but she always had that beautiful smile on her face, her light still shining bright. The night she died, I knew she was going to die; I couldn't sleep, and I felt like something was wrong. It was the next night she came to me in a dream. She smiled at me, and I woke up abruptly. It felt so real, but it scared me. The night after, I dreamed of her again, and this time when she smiled, I said, "Where did you go? I thought you were gone forever." She replied, "I haven't left. I will always be with you."

Even now, when I go through dark times, my grandma comes to me in a dream and smiles at me, and she always says the same thing, "I will always be with you, I'm still here." I wake up feeling peaceful because it feels the same way it did when she was alive in her physical body. It feels the same as when she just passed on that night, when she came to me for the first time.

Years later, my cousin died unexpectedly from a very aggressive cancer. I was working away at my computer, and my jewelry box fell off the dresser. I thought perhaps it was simply too close to the edge. A few moments later, I heard, "Watch over her." It was about my niece Masynn, who was one at the time.

I started to realize that there was something much more inside of me and underneath the illusions of this world we are living in. The dreams started, and then I began to hear more often inner guidance, and then as I began to meditate more and get into the float tank, words and writing and seeing began to be a daily thing. I started to know things about people, and I realized it was a gift to help others. I saw more than what people showed me. It was like I could see right into them and some of them straight through. Lately, the gifts of knowing, hearing, and seeing are hard as sometimes you don't want to know certain things. Once you open that channel of intuition, it is there and never goes away, like the way someone will say something or look at you in a certain way, and you get a stomach pain because you already know what they are going to say isn't going to be good. An intuitive feeling, that gut feeling is never wrong. Yes, a lot like that.

Heal yourself

When I finally left a big agency to head back to New York City to take another agency job, I knew in my heart of hearts it wouldn't last. As I was beginning to realize that I need to be out on my own, the universe kicked me out onto the street to find my way. I lost my job in Brooklyn and began meditating daily, and I was introduced to essential oils by my amazing esthetician. Like most of us, my identity and worth were tied to my job and what I had, and without my job, I was at a loss for knowing who I was or what I wanted. I went on a serious seeking mission for the next six years.

I began taking classes, reading everything I could get my hands on about healing, and I started practicing Reiki. I upped my meditation from thirty minutes to an hour. I got into the float tank monthly. I was all in on my path to embody peace and feel at home in my presence. As I stepped onto a new part of my path and started going within, I then entered a turbulent time on my journey. I got sick. At the same time, my marriage fell apart, and it was apparent that it was now time to let it go. I was very sick with adrenal fatigue and was physically the sickest I had been since beating cancer at eighteen. I was dizzy every day for two years. For 730 days, I was dizzy and found basic life things to be incredibly hard to deal with. What followed for the next two years was physically, mentally, and emotionally crippling because no one had answers for what was wrong with me.

This created incredible anxiety and a fear of accomplishing basic life tasks. Those two years were humbling, but they also taught me to be present and to let go. I was literally in a holding pattern. I went into full surrender to divine spirit's highest vision for my path. As time passed, I spent all my time working on me and healing. I had been in an abusive relationship, and I was out of alignment with myself. I had tons of tests and changed my diet. They thought I had vertigo. I didn't.

When I left that relationship, I felt better in a week. How crazy is that? The mind-body-spirit connection became very clear to me. Everything is connected. I began to expand my consciousness through meditation, being creative, and working on my self-love. I started using tools such as float tanks, binaural beats, tantra, and emotional freedom technique (EFT) in conjunction with many other tools. I dove into finding my balance, healing, and uncovering my truths so that I could eventually begin to help other souls find their balance, heal, and uncover their truths. Once I was balanced and in flow, I took off on my biggest journey of all time, moving from the East Coast back home to LA.

Sometimes you just have to burn it down.

Exactly, burn it down. We must burn it all down to the ground. Burn all the limiting beliefs that we think are ours, down to the ground. Vanquish them. All those thoughts that incite fear within us. These limiting thoughts that create false constructs around us, within us and limit our pure potential.

Do you think fear is real? It isn't. It's just a bunch of limiting beliefs we've been programmed to believe that we think are helping us, but in essence, they are holding us back. Limiting us. To think is to feel. Fear = Control. Fear and failure probably are the two biggest control factors in our minds. As Joe Vitale says in *The Awakened Millionaire*, failure is just feedback to continue working at it. Day in and day out, we must keep building it. We only fail when we give up on our passion and our purpose.

When my marriage started falling apart, it was another turning point for me. As I was struggling against what was and what I thought

I wanted, I felt completely lost and frustrated. Things were not working. Clearly, my self-love wasn't strong. Clearly, I had limiting beliefs. I felt disconnected from who I truly was and what I truly wanted. It took me a long time to see this, but it was as if it had been there all along. You know how you can drive the same road or listen to the same song, but you never really see something or hear something until it's that right time, and then you can't believe you were so unaware, so unconscious, for so long? How is that possible? It was right there the entire time. It is similar to trying to connect with someone, but because you are on two different vibrational frequencies, the messages cannot be received and exchanged.

I found myself in the car with my mom, ready to run some errands, and next thing I knew, I started sobbing and could not hold back the tears. I started talking about one of my closest friends, who was living this amazing life. I felt like a failure. Everything I had was falling apart. My mom looked over at me, not knowing what to say.

Later that night, I started thinking about what I wanted. Did I even know? Could I tell the difference between what I truly wanted and what I had been programmed to want? As I slowly started to think about it all, maybe I didn't need to be married. Did I need to look a certain way? Maybe I didn't need to make tons and tons of money at a shit slave job I hated where the people didn't respect me. Maybe the business I had built wasn't for me anymore. I felt lost. Things had gotten to the breaking point, but still, I couldn't see my way out of it. I didn't want to let go, so I kept holding on. My fear owned me. I felt stuck, heavy. It was hard to do anything. As a new business owner and with the stress of cash flow and my failing marriage, I was feeling so tired and weak a lot of days.

That year while on a trip to Amsterdam, one minute, I was fine and having a great time, and the next, I was dizzy and could hardly walk. It was as if a switch had been turned on, and I felt physically awful. Shortly after that, I went for a handful of tests at the hospital. The doctor said that perhaps it was vertigo. Who knew? Certainly not me. This went on for a year. Every day was the same; I would wake up and feel drunk and dizzy and could hardly function. Then it went on for two years. Things that were easy like walking my dog became a chore. The hardest part was how vague my doctor was. It could go away or maybe not. There was no rhyme or reason to when it was really bad and other days when it was a little better. This went on day in and day out for two years—about 730 days of feeling like I couldn't live my life or do basic things. My type-A personality, the always on the go, running five miles a week, always working... was coming to an end. I felt betrayed by my body.

To be honest, I was nearly thirty-six, and I was fucking pissed! Even as this was happening, I refused to slow down and give up. I continued to fight against my experience to pretend that I was okay. As uncomfortable as it was, I kept running, I kept working, I kept rock climbing, I kept on doing, I wouldn't let up. Well, rock climbing in such a shit state was pretty badass, but I was also being disrespectful to my body.

After six months of this, I just gave up. Some days I lay in bed all day depressed, wondering why this was happening, and other days I carried on as if I wasn't going to fall over in public like a drunk person. One day I ventured to Whole Foods, and as I was shopping, the dizziness got so bad, I had to stop walking. My mind kicked on high and loud. The anxiety set in. I have never had anxiety in my life. It felt so powerful, like a tidal wave knocking me down. I thought, "Shit, how will I drive home? I am all alone. Who will help me? How will I finish shopping?"

I felt tears coming on. I felt powerless. I felt like a fucking victim, and that pissed me off. My mind was spinning out in full panic mode. At that moment, because I had been meditating for a few years at this point, I became aware, actually aware of my awareness. "NO! These are just thoughts. I will not indulge them. I will not feed them. I will not attach to them. I am no victim. I am in control of me." I took a few deep breaths, and I thought, "I am almost thirty-six years old. I have figured out everything up until this point, everything, all of it. This is no different."

Needless to say, I made it to the checkout, made it to the car, and made it home. Everything was okay. All we need to know is that we will figure it out, whatever it is, and if we need help, we need to ask. It is a simple concept, but how often have we allowed ourselves to be that victim and pull out our victim card? All we need to remember is that we need to be aware, conscious of our breath, in and out, and keep taking steps forward. In this case, if I needed to crawl, I would have crawled. When things feel hard, we just have to remember to keep moving and rest when we need to rest.

Lastly, all the limiting beliefs we have that control our reality, we need to burn them down. Burn it all down and start again. Limiting beliefs are false constructs that stop us from living out our full potential. When we indulge our limiting beliefs, they stop us from being present and from having the full experience of what we are being shown. Why is this happening for me? What are the lessons here? I realized that I could move my power to the front and move my fear to the back quite simply. Something the awareness of mediation showed me. I was fucking winning! I started asking, What is the spirit showing me? What am I learning from this experience instead of being so caught up in my feelings?

We are all addicted.

No two people in this entire universe are having the same experience. Yes, we will feel similar things, but no one is you.

Something that barely affects one person will destroy another. Our bodies and minds can only take so much stress and trauma, and then we begin to check out, use defense mechanisms, and do our best to survive. We find ourselves addicted to the stories we tell in our minds that suffocate us late at night. Addicted to things that make us feel better. Addicted to the familiar even if it's bad for us. Addicted to running from ourselves. The way to break free from anything is to be honest. To ask for help. To begin to create a safe space for yourself by running towards you in every view. Make a promise to no longer abandon yourself.

Abandoning your feelings creates shame. Abandoning you creates shame. Abandoning your needs creates shame. Abandoning yourself makes you feel unsafe. Abandoning you makes you feel weak and powerless. This creates anxiety and depression because you're running. This cycle goes round and round until you can start being fully present.

Stand still until you're ready to begin again. The secret that you may or may not know is that there is no shame in being a mess. There is no shame in struggling. There is no shame in who you are, where you've been, or how you're doing your best to find your way home to you and your best self. Now that you know this, simply acknowledge you. Acknowledge your feelings. Accept you and where you are.

Make a promise never to abandon yourself again. You don't have to do anything but acknowledge and accept you, simply put a hand on your heart and be present with yourself.

By embodying your truth of why you feel you need something is the way to begin to stand in your truth. To bring awareness to something takes its power away.

Watch your entire life change just by running towards you in every view and by being true.

Start turning the volume down on the stories and chaos and turn the volume up on your awareness and dedication to you.

Turn the volume up on your power and your ability to be present when you're uncomfortable.

You are worthy just because you exist. No one and nothing can change that.

In addition to the addictions we live in, we often dim down for most of our lives.

I know, the first time you felt embarrassed or got bullied or made fun of, you dimmed down a little. Or when you grew up in a codependent family with controlling parents, and you realized to survive and keep the peace, everyone came before you and your needs, so you turned off your needs to adapt and survive. You don't need much. You're not important. Only as you ignore yourself and abandon yourself in the name of others, it gets harder and harder to stuff the anger down.

When you've always felt weird, wild, and different and felt like no one ever truly saw you, you watered yourself down a little more and adapted.

When they told you that you take things too seriously, or you watered yourself down, maybe you started doing drugs to numb out because you started to believe that you were too much. You were tired of thinking and feeling alone, so you disconnected from yourself and the world around you.

There are so many things and so many reasons and experiences of why we water ourselves down and adapt. You adapted the best you knew how to.

Remember when you had an abandonment wound, so you felt needy in your relationships, ashamed to ask for what you need? So you told yourself you needed nothing. So day in and day out, you moved between desperation and anxiety and who-gives-a-fuck shut down and closed. Chasing and running, hiding, and shutting down, stuck in a cycle of fuck.

I see you, you gorgeous soul, because I used to water me down and adapt to survive and preserve me at all costs.

We all adapt and water ourselves down, and we go round and round, one day realizing that we can be true in the view.

You are strong, and you survived, but now it's time to thrive and dive in.

The world needs the real you. Are you ready?

I see you, and I love you. The world is waiting for you. Are you ready for you?

Embracing the darkness and surfing your shadow

We now realize that everyone has a shadow side, and everyone has pain and patterns that control our behaviors. Another side of the struggle is resting when we have not built a sacred space or started to show our true face in this space. We resist. We resist looking and asking the questions. We resist looking at our baggage in the closet that we don't want to heal, sort through, and let go of. We resist feeling, and that gets us into trouble. We resist letting go, which further complicates. In all truth, no one gives us a manual, so it takes years to learn how to embody our true essence. It kind of reminds me of rock climbing. We have different mountains to climb, and what works for one may not work for another. I remember someone who had a longer reach than me would give me some beta, beta is how to conquer a climb, but for me, because my body and strengths are different, it wouldn't work for me. Just like something can barely affect one person and destroy another person. Some climbs and issues are easier to conquer than others.

We learn to figure much out for ourselves. While listening to others' stories and truths can help spark our own, we have to do our own inner work as no one can do it for us. Ultimately, we resist, we resist a lot of things, but when we stop resisting, we can begin to surf through everything.

The old saying, when we stop resisting, it stops persisting. When we fight, it keeps coming. When we accept and just be, most things will fall out of our holographic reality. When we have the courage to claim our darkness and integrate it into our light, things become alright. It's no longer a fight. You can shift and lift your vibration at will when you learn to be still. When you claim your darkness and your light and give up the fight, you realize you are a sinner and a saint. I know I never said that I ain't. What people don't get is that once you accept yourself and are whole, you aren't concerned with what others thing or when others judge because you know that you make mistakes because you own them. You are no longer trying to be perfect because you are whole. You don't need to be anything other than what you are.

Most of my life, I tried to be a perfectionist because I felt like I had something to prove, and I needed some serious healing back then. I felt the pressure of wanting to be perfect because somehow thinking that achieving would fill me up and help me close that hole in my heart, but it just kept coming apart. It wasn't healing.

I became acquainted with my darkness as a child. Some days I remember floating through life feeling invisible. My inner world felt like absolute chaos. Yes, there were moments of happiness, but the majority of the time, I felt everything everyone else was feeling, and then I had my own stuff. It always felt as if the storm would never end and that things were just happening to me. I was a tiny ship being blown around in a sea of constant disaster.

I spent decades feeling depressed, sad, angry, confused, and anxious. I had no tools and no idea what to do. I felt powerless. It was quite honestly the worst feeling until as the years passed, I found tools, I surrendered, and I stopped running.

Our inner worlds are a maze of twists and turns, and then we are out in the world doing our best as we begin to experience life inside and out in the world as we interact with others, further adding to and having to make sense of things that we experience.

All my life, people have told me that I seem so happy and that I have so much light I bring and show to the world, but what the awakened ones know it is the polarity of who we are. We have light because, on the other end of the spectrum, it is that we have embraced our darkness. By far, what I am about to say has been the biggest growth and catalyst for my self-empowerment, and I hope it will be for you as well.

If you only take one thing away, please hear this because even this is enough to transform you in ways you have never dreamed of.

You have to get to the point where you trust yourself and your experience. Over a decade of meditation has taught me to know and embrace my patterns' pain and rabbit holes. Be at home wandering your rabbit holes in the dark before you go deeper. You don't want to be, or stay, a sleeper. Understand your patterns' fears and past pain;

otherwise, you drown in your rain. When I say your, you are the creator of your entire experience. You can stop feeling bad anytime you want to. I know because I did, and a lot of people do it. You have to get to the point where you are at home with your negative emotions, to the point where you don't feel overwhelmed. You don't even feel that bad anymore, because your attitude is more of trust and you say fuck it, lean into it. Lean into your edge. You got this. You know you can handle anything. You get to a point where you don't empower your emotions. You learn to witness; everything doesn't require a response. Begin to be curious, trust everything, and let go. You don't have to grab onto everything in your mind. Let everything pass through because there is no you. You are the watcher, the pure awareness, the listener. Simply begin to work on witnessing.

Every traumatic event or hurt we experience adds a story to the fabric of our being and carries an energy signature we carry forward. Our energy attracts. Our energy speaks. Our energy gives us access or denies us. We align and get what we want, or we don't. We often feel so much confusion around why things are happening or how. At first, we don't even realize that we have the power to attract or move energy or do anything about anything in our lives. When we do realize mostly, we think we can get what we want by doing. That's partly true, but there are other components to the equation.

The other day someone online posted about being sick. I mentioned powerful energy tools for healing, and the person said I have been so busy I can't get into that mindset to think about healing my energy. We subscribe to many illusions and false conclusions. I thought to myself, You don't have time to think about energy. That's all there is—energy and now. There is nothing else. Energy doesn't lie. When

I found myself sick with cancer or exhausted from adrenal fatigue or stuck, healing my energy made these things nonexistent.

Energy is everything.

The stories we tell carry an energy signature and bring us more or less or something. The emotions we carry are energy. The intentions and actions we put forth in the world are energy. It's all energy. Are the stories and energy you are carrying from day to day empowering you? That is the question we have to ask if we want to be empowered and hack our consciousness. It's the question we have to ask if we want to architect our reality. What is your energy bringing you? The world will reflect your inner world to you. Do you take the time to evaluate and rewrite the stories you carry as you evolve to evolve with you and empower you? Do you understand the impact of the stories and energy you are carrying?

You are the lock, and the key, do you see? The reality we create is a combination of beliefs, stories, emotions, and energy, further amplified by the balance of masculine/action - feminine/being. We hold the power to hack our consciousness through energy work.

You are questioning, and you are answering. You are chained, and you are liberated. You are chaos and calm; you are the one who drops the bomb.

The moment you decide to surrender to the flow but to be in control of harnessing your darkness and utilizing tools for healing, you become incredibly powerful, awake, and aware, and it will take you everywhere.

The moment you empower you, the view will change. Watch things rearrange.

Declare out loud as you become initiated if you haven't already, and if you have already declared out loud, declare now a deeper commitment to be more empowered, especially if you have been holding back in certain places and spaces. Give yourself permission to be empowered. To heal. To walk through the stories and rewrite them. To understand your energy and how to manage it.

Make yourself at home within your dark, not because you plan to stay, but because it's not going to sway you any longer. You are simply getting stronger.

The only way to free your emotions is to feel them. Breathe into them at every twist and turn. They don't have to burn you any longer. You're growing stronger. You are safe to feel because it is real. You are safe to acknowledge your emotions. You are safe to be alone with your emotions. How often do you acknowledge your emotions and feel them, thank them, and free them? Are you still running from you?

I know it is often late at night when we are putting up that fight, we can feel hopeless or sad or like we just can't take it anymore. We think we want our life to end, but we just want the pain to end, to send these feelings away.

Breathe deeply and feel. Know what's real.

I declare I am no longer holding onto any negative emotions. I will feel them and free them. I do not need to hold onto them, obsess about them. All will be well. All is well.

These feelings are just feelings. My mind is a projection. It's just reflection, but I am in control. Under the noise, I can find poise. I can breathe, sit still until I am ready to begin again.

As you acknowledge that you are in control and that the stories and attachments to this moment are within your control, you are now letting go. Any thoughts you keep thinking and any negative emotion you now want to hold onto, let them move through the view so you can be born anew.

As you acknowledge how powerful you are, you use your mind to visualize everything around you is now falling like a mist. Insist that everything disappear, everything that was near was powered by fear. As the world around you disappears, you now turn your awarenesses to within.

You are no longer scared, or angry, or sad. Those feelings are fading just as the world around you faded at your will. Your visualization of what is and what you want it to be is within your mind, and you are finding your way.

These feelings are like unwanted ghosts, but because you are so much magic, you banish them at will. If you still feel sad and bad and negative, simply let it stay. Emotions have so much to say when they stay, and we need to listen.

During this time, it is a time for you to realize how powerful you are. You are in control. There is nothing for you to fear. Make yourself at home in your dark. Everything you feel and everything you experience is for you. Nothing is happening to you, but for you. Everything is a catalyst for change, just to rearrange.

Breathe into your power, embrace it, and face it. Breathe into your strength. You always figure things out. Face it and embrace it. Lay down your resistance to going against this moment and suffering. Embrace it and face it. See beyond this illusion in your mind. Are the stories true? Is this an absolute truth or a relative truth? Try and stay open and objective. Don't hold on so tightly.

Will you give yourself permission to accept, integrate, and surrender to who you truly are?

IF YOU ARE, SAY THIS OUT LOUD:

I claim the darkness and the shadow that lives within. This choice is of the highest initiation. Facing and embracing my shadow frees me from illusions and false conclusions.

I claim the white and light that lives within. As I burn bright, I have sight. This choice is of the highest integration as I surrender to shine my way through into a new view. I am born true.

I claim the passion, purpose, and pleasure that lives within me. This choice brings me into alignment, and I am forever illuminated. I choose empowerment. This holds the key to my now, and how I see and how I can be.

If you are traversing your darkness, please take these words into your heart and let them transform your feelings on feeling negative emotion. Please let these words comfort, awaken, and empower you.

Our decisions make us and break us. It is of no concern, you will learn, whether you think you are up or down or the wrong way round, you will be found. As conscious expansion happens, all of our decisions, actions, and energy bring us along the path. Right or wrong is an illusion. All paths converge into one true place, and you will show your true face and be replaced by who you truly are as you will have traveled far.

When we question it all, we will inevitably fall. When we face our inner deep, we are no longer asleep. When we no longer decide to abide or hide, we turn the tide. Own and honor your darkness that smashes into your light that you think isn't right. Transcend everything until you reach your still point in the night, brilliant and bright, so much light. Resistance is part of the path. There are levels to this shit.

As you begin to integrate the lost, stolen, hidden pieces, the old you is dying. As you give yourself permission to begin this mission with your full awareness and as you fully surrender to your consciousness, which is expanding at a rapid rate, you are being born from form and function to magic and magnificence.

Emotions are a part of this human experience. When we have learned to trust ourselves and our experience, we can see certain things for what they truly are.

No matter how you choose to feel, see, react or be, all is a catalyst for your conscious expansion. You're on your way, so don't delay in worrying or hurrying. Just be you in this view.

Consciously let the negativity leave by letting it breathe. Don't let it deceive, then weave your magic.

LIFE. DEATH. REBIRTH. Over and over. Life, death, rebirth. Everything has a cycle and a rhythm. Everything is born, sustained, dies, and then is transformed.

Peace, Power, and Presence is your birthright. We are saying good-bye to unnecessary struggling. Struggle is part of the process, but it is not everything.

Peace- I feel peace, I release, all that ways me down, I have been found. I feel peace. When was the last time you felt peaceful? Peace is accessible in an instant through the redirection of energy. You were made to move energy. You have just forgotten. Peace is accessible through your breath and mind. Find your way, and stay there. Stay and lay still. Even in the midst of chaos in a public space, your true face is peace as you cease to worry or fear what will be near, my dear. Close your eyes and breathe. Relieve your body and mind of any stress that was there (Breathe.) As I begin to drum, your mind, body, and spirit will synchronize into splendor as you surrender.

Power- I have no more fear. My power is here. I must trust. I trust, which is a must.

When was the last time you felt powerful? See that moment. Feel that moment. Let your body connect to that moment. Let the energy and strength of your power move through your body. See this light moving through you.

Presence- I live in the now; I will not bow to the past or future. I am present.

RESISTANCE - Have you claimed your dark and your light? I am a sinner and a saint. I never said that I ain't. All is but a mirror for us to see. Have you integrated your shadow side into your light?

Chapter 6

POWERFUL TOOLS
FOR HEALING

Healing is returning home to who you truly are. It's aligning with your inner rhythm. It's about being rebalanced. It's about aligning your mind, body, and energy. When was the last time you made time to honor the healing that you need? We spend so much time running from ourselves and situations and people and things that need tending to. We are all a chaotic, beautiful mess, and our humanness is so amazing. Run towards you in every view. It is about seeing.

The power of 3

There are three classes of people: Those who see. Those who see when they are shown. Those who do not see. – Leonardo da Vinci

Can you see yet? Do you want to see? Will you see? If not yet, when? Quite often, we don't see with our eyes. I have never seen that much with my eyes, but more, I have felt with my spirit and my heart. I have felt the truth and seen through the illusions, and I know you have too.

How do we see, and how can we be free?

SOUND HEALING

My first experience with sound healing was at a group sound bath at a spiritual event at a friend's house in California. I was intrigued. At this point, I had been meditating daily for fifteen years. I had been into the float tank about ten times. I had read book after book and taken class after class. I was seeking all the healing tools available. As I stated earlier, I had been working on healing for decades. After the first sound bath, there were a few more group sound baths I attended, and I started to understand more and more through my experience that the power of sound could shift vibrational states, but it wasn't until I received a private sound bath that I was blown away. This time during a private sound bath in a park during the day, the sound healer used tuning forks and drumming in addition to crystal singing bowls. I was blown away.

That morning I wasn't particularly in the best mood and had a lot on my mind, but when I lay down on the blanket on the grass, I didn't have any expectations, and I wasn't sure what I would feel or see. What happened next as I drifted in and out of consciousness, I was blown away. I began to see past life memories. I heard guidance. The guidance I received about something was going to come to pass came true a few weeks later. I saw powerful imagery of myself being cleansed and reborn.

Most importantly, I felt amazing. I felt high and happy and balanced, and that whatever was weighing me down was now cleared away. I remember leaving that day and feeling similar to how I felt the first time I floated. Light and airy, happy and high. I felt as if I was the best version of myself and all inner resistance had been cleared away, and I was free to live my life.

As soon as I experienced this, I wanted to learn and share it with the world. I have always known that I wanted to help other souls, and I had been through sharing my experiences through video and writing, but this I felt so deeply on a whole other level. I became so excited and started reading all I could about the power of sound healing, and I began taking lessons with different healers. A few months later, I began practicing on friends. As I began practicing, my work began evolving. Clearing space, holding space, bringing custom oil mixes into private sessions. Utilizing Reiki and tuning forks. Drumming and using crystal singing bowls.

As I began meeting with clients, it was fascinating to hear that everyone was experiencing something different but powerful. One of my friends said, "It felt like a sober acid trip." Another said, " I could feel all my worries going down the drain, and I felt brand new, and I felt so much love, like I was being held and lifted."

Sound Healing can help with the following:
- Clearing energetic blocks.
- Depression.
- Anxiety.
- Sleep issues.
- Managing stress.
- PTSD.

Sound healing can help you move into a state of trance. Release resistance. Increase awareness.

MOVE INTO A STATE OF TRANCE.

RELEASE RESISTANCE.

INCREASE AWARENESS.

ALIGN MIND, BODY, and SPIRIT.

HEAL THROUGH SIGHT and SOUND, and YOU WILL BE FOUND.

Chapter 7

PERCEPTION — WHO ARE YOU? YOUR FOCUS IS YOUR FREEDOM — WHERE IS YOUR FOCUS?

Is your identity built on what has happened to you? Is healing also not clinging to this idea of your identity of what happened to you. Congruency allows for alignment and protection of your time-space energy and inner sacred space.

How do you spend your time? Is it fighting with people on Facebook? Are you taking time to love you?

Know yourself and what you need. Nothing is more important than knowing what you want, knowing where you have been, and where you want to go.

Even if you aren't exactly sure, you can still have some ideas about where you want to go. Setting sacred intentions and powerful new beliefs is a way to attract that which you are becoming.

Every day you can take one to two minutes daily to be in control of you. In the whirlwind of constant technology, outside energies, practice surrendering to who you are. Practice controlling your inner dialogue despite external chaos. As the wind blows around, it will surround you, and without a sound, ground into your experience. Take a few deep breaths, and then say mentally or out loud, "I am present in this moment. I am grateful for this moment. I accept whatever this moment brings. I accept my feelings." These statements begin to shift your awareness, your energy, and move you into a state of power, peace, and presence. You decide what you allow in your sacred space. It doesn't mean that you don't feel bad or that you don't have thoughts that lower your vibration or that you don't feel inner chaos, but you can begin to direct your inner experience to shift your outer experience. When you begin to do this, you will start to realize that you don't have time to feel bad all the time. You don't have the energy to fight against who you truly are.

Chapter 8

SACRED SPACE: BUILDING SACRED SPACE AND SHOWING YOUR TRUE FACE IN THIS PLACE

WHAT IS SACRED SPACE AND UNDERSTANDING WHY YOU NEED TO BUILD IT CONSCIOUSLY

What is sacred space, and how do we build it? We subconsciously build sacred space over our lives. We expand and learn boundaries and stop accepting less than we deserve. We start honoring who we are and being truer in the view. To consciously build sacred space is a powerful thing. Consciously, carefully, consistently consider and cultivate your sacred space. In this crazy place, erase, embrace, and interlace your true face.

Sacred space is a mental and energetic embodiment that is yours that no one can decide to change or affect. Sacred space is a deep and strong connection to self. Building sacred space is the key to your freedom and empowerment. It is built through practices, rituals, and acknowledgment of self. It is a decision, a permission, and an endless flow of pouring love back into one's self. It is a space you build over time that keeps you in a state of empowerment and peace. You understand how to release what is no longer yours. What was never you, what was never true in this view. You are free to be you.

I noticed when I began meditating back when I was twenty-seven, after losing my job and feeling as though I lost my identity, which was a total illusion that little by little, I became more aware. I became calmer. I became more of me. I could see clearer. I was becoming more empowered the more I sat and meditated. I was beginning to surrender moment by moment. I began having deeper conversations with divine spirit and my inner being. I began shifting away from a victim mindset of thinking that external and internal things could rock me so much. I began to decide what was important and what was illusion. I began to turn down the volume and color on things that used to rock me. I began to turn the volume and focus up on me and my inner world and whatever would empower me. I began to decide how to move energy in my space and release attachments to as many things as I could. I began to feel a gratitude, a love, and a sense of watching and less reacting as I replaced who I was pretending to be. I started to realize that nothing was happening *to* me but *for* me and that the universe was simply responding to my vibrational frequency. Hence the reason like attracts like, and yes, we still experience contrast. Contrast, as in people are still going to be triggered by you and you by them. I started to become aware of where I invested and focused my energy, as well. I started to become even more sensitive to other people's energy at first, and then I began to learn how to ground and shield and watch.

My meditation practice started as five minutes a day, and at some point, that first year, it increased up to an hour or more. That was many years ago. To this day, I have added more rituals and energy tools into how I build, protect, and manipulate energy in my sacred space. Sacred space takes time to build, and the more why questions we ask helps us to build it. The more we look at our patterns, the more empowered we are. The more we turn inward, the more strength we gain. The more we can simply be aware and watch, the more empowered we are. The more we learn how to hold our vibrational frequency, the stronger our sacred space is.

I constantly have downloads on things. I was dancing one morning and deeply connecting to my self in my body and my breathing. I heard the energy has to move, and we have to move how we want. When the world is moving at a rapid speed, sacred space is moving to your own song, which will never be wrong. Can you hear it? What does your inner rhythm and alignment feel like when you are connected and moving at a pace that feels right to you while living in your sacred space?

I started with meditation as my first tool for empowerment and building sacred space. Then I began using other tools such as sensory deprivation, plant medicine, EFT, and Kundalini, and my energy, thoughts, reactions, and actions changed. I began to flow with grace and ease, and there wasn't much that could displease me. Sometimes things still bothered me but not like in the past. These things didn't last. My foundation was growing stronger mentally, and energetically I was becoming stronger. I am strong, and I grow stronger every day. You are strong, and you grow stronger every day. You probably have no idea how much stronger you are than you think you are. You have to remember that every challenge put in your path is just a catalyst for change as you exchange one version of who you are for another.

Sacred space is built as fear fades away. Sacred space is built as you begin to empower and disempower things. It starts with building a strong foundation as you begin to evaluate your beliefs and thoughts. Most get stuck here hoping to stop thinking negative thoughts, but it isn't that simple.

This is why energy tools are powerful. You can shift mentally as you shift energetically. Shifting energetically brings you to another frequency where you can access guidance you may not have had on a lower vibrational frequency. This is why I fell in love with sound healing and Kundalini yoga because it doesn't matter what you are thinking. As you listen to mantras, do a movement and use your breath, or even hear the sound of the instruments, you will be transformed. I have so many people tell me after I work on them through a sound healing and Reiki session that things that were keeping them stuck mentally have been cleared away just by listening. They feel so empowered for the first time in their lives, and all they did was listen.

As you raise your energetic frequency, your thoughts and emotions change as well. We only have so much time on this planet, so much energy, and so much focus, and the more you can build your sacred space you take with you everywhere, you can be happier, live the life you want, and feel more peace and freedom and less suffocating by your thoughts and interactions with others.

We are often fearful a lot of the time because of past trauma that has happened to us, and it stays stored in our bodies. We continue to have many of the same thoughts, stories, and themes around the things that have happened to us. Those patterns stay trapped unless we use energy work to clear them out. We go out in the world, and we begin to interact with other souls, and we let these interactions affect us sometimes positively and quite often negatively. How many times have you woken up in a great mood only to have an interaction, and then have your mood changed in an instant? This very thing is disempowering. As you build sacred space, you start to understand that you, as the alchemist, can bend, break, shift, and lift things at will, but first, you have to be still, believe, and then you have to receive the guidance and embody it.

No one can see our mental space from the outside. Other people do feel our energy intentions and patterns we carry in our energetic fields, why we attract certain experiences, and why we manifest certain outcomes.

Building sacred space is a combination of pulling your foundation apart; understanding your patterns and reasons why you do what you do; healing these patterns; setting powerful intentions; deeply connecting with self; and using tools to heal and balance. Giving yourself permission to consciously move, breathe, create, surrender flow, and move and create your reality the way you want to.

Chapter 9

YOU MUST BUILD
YOUR SACRED SPACE

*ACTIONABLE STEPS TO BUILD SACRED SPACE AND SHOW
YOUR TRUE FACE IN THIS SPACE. HOW TO SHIFT INTO
EMPOWERMENT AND ALIGNMENT WITH SOURCE*

The actionable steps to building sacred space—deciding because once you decide, it's going to happen. We often tell stories about how we need to do this and that, but mostly it's about clearing away what isn't serving or helping us to be empowered. We are already everything.

* Decide. What we often fail to realize is that we are powerful, and even the simple decision to decide carries a big weight to start a momentum and fuel things to happen. So just decide. In this moment, knowing what you want to do and deciding is going to feel good, and you are going to feel the universe hear your call. You are going to feel your ancestors and guides, angels, and the infinite energy and consciousness of the universe and that in which you are will begin to move once you choose. You will feel lighter, and the energy within and without a doubt will begin to support you. You are divinely loved,

guided and protected, and never misdirected. Trust and decide, abide by your decision, and let the energy shift and lift you into alignment. When you decide to build sacred space, you are deciding to love, honor, and protect your mental and energetic space and erase all that no longer resonates.

* Give yourself permission. Permission is an acknowledgment, it is an intention, it is power, and it is setting a deep intention to honor and love yourself. Often, we have nonverbal or verbal commitments, conscious and unconscious, to not honor ourselves or love ourselves or connect with ourselves. Every time we say yes when we want to say no. Every time we don't give ourselves what we need mentally, emotionally, or physically, we are not honoring ourselves. Every time we ignore our needs, we disempower ourselves over and over again.

This is a pattern in our energetic field that we are broadcasting to the world. We then wonder why nothing is changing or why we feel stuck. Without permission, we repeat the same things over and over. Permission is powerful. Know what you want and give yourself permission and watch how this small intentional thing called permission shifts your power and energy instantly. You may even feel instantly lighter because you have been weighed down by so much inside and outside. We often adhere to expectations we put on ourselves and that others put on us.

* When you decide and give yourself permission, you are making a deep commitment to connect with yourself every moment, every day, deeply and to listen to what your intuition is telling you. When you give permission and commit, you are on your way.

* Honor your practice every single day. My practice is usually 35 minutes to an hour every day, meditation, dance, yoga, kriyas, practicing tantra and making love to myself, talking to myself, loving myself, brief or deep energy work through Reiki, Kundalini, and sound. Your practice can be as long or short as you want, but you must decide, give yourself permission, and honor it consistently. The more you connect with yourself, the more empowered, intuitive, and peaceful you will feel. It's hard to have anxiety when you are honoring and listening to your body, mind, and heart. It's harder for you to feel stressed when you are taking time for you. Every day I deeply connect with myself, thus I know myself, and I listen to myself. Every time you engage in the practice of connecting with yourself, you are building a foundation that cannot be penetrated by the outside world as your primary relationship is with yourself. I used to read this all the time, but I didn't see actionable steps to manifest this reality. Additionally, you need to review your beliefs, thoughts, and energy daily, and shift if you want to expand.

When building sacred space, you are evaluating your beliefs and thoughts to empower you, the true you, not the you that acts from wounds and defense mechanisms and ego protection. You activate your awareness on a soul level. You begin deep connecting with yourself for knowledge and intuition, and you reclaim your empowerment. Through deep connection, you tune into you, and you begin to let more self-love flow, which is the root of all the issues. You learn to disempower mainly everything outside of you. You stop the round and round because you have been found. You are so tuned in to the now and yourself that your vibration is incredibly high, and you are less affected by negativity and what is.

* Know when to rest and when to do

There is much confusion in the practice of the embodiment of masculine and feminine energy. There is much destruction in relationships when we don't understand polarity. Knowing when to do and be is power, and when you are in your power, you embody alignment.

* Making love to yourself and prioritizing your self-pleasure

Enjoying and receiving pleasure is about loving yourself. So many people want more but struggle to receive all the abundance already in their lives. You can start small by practicing receiving everything that comes your way every day.

* Creating boundaries and saying, "Fuck no," to toxic people and situations that threaten to feed and drain you

All shifts are mental and energetic. When was the last time you took a deep dive at your thoughts and asked why you are thinking that? Was it a past thing that happened? Did someone tell you it was true, and you bought into it as part of your foundation? Where are our foundations created from? The outside world influences everything about who we think we are, especially if we never self-reflect or heal or decide for ourselves what is true for us. How much of our foundations were created by outside influences? How much of your foundation have you considered, thought about, and decided on?

Do you feel that your mental space is strong? How often are you stressed out? Do you feel fragile out in the world like your peace of mind is predicated on outside things? How often do you allow others to disrupt your inner peace? How often can you stay open without expectations of how it should be versus how it is? How often do you repeat patterns? How often are you disappointed? How often do you have to isolate yourself when trying to process things? How often do you hide from intimacy or conflict? How often do you shut down when you don't feel safe? Safe in your body, safe in your life?

Here are a few questions to help you begin the process of building a stronger foundation in your mental space. It is crazy how long we believe and think the same things and have similar experiences until we think differently or change our energetics and foundation.

At any moment, we can decide to tell different stories and, in addition, use energy tools to break energetic patterns stored in our fields and expand into greater consciousness and awareness, which leads to giving fewer fucks and enjoying more of our moments without expectations.

Are your thoughts empowering you or disempowering you? If I had to guess, it may be all disempowering a lot of the time, or you are very empowered, but there are a few things still holding you back that you may be actively working through. Do your thoughts empower you in your environment? Do you feel safe? Do you feel loved by yourself and others? Do you feel as though you belong here, and you have more than enough? Do you feel connected to your inner being? Do you feel divinely connected to your source and converse on them daily?

For instance, examples of empowering thoughts: Everything happens *for* me, not *to* me. There are lessons in all things that happen, and these contrasting events are for my benefit. I always get what I want because I am powerful. I ask, believe, and receive.

Your foundation creates your reality, as I am sure you have heard this many times, but until we pull all the pieces apart, it is hard to see where and what, to see what needs healing, shifting, and lifting. I have found that looking at who I thought I was, who I am, what I want, and where I found myself feeling stuck is a really interesting and beautiful process that I enjoy. I have always loved learning and watching and feeling into things. Life is a beautiful mystery, and some things we may never know, but others can be more apparent when we just look with our eyes and an open heart.

What is your foundation creating in your life and your inner world? What would you love to change, and what feels good?

Chapter 10

EMPTY YOUR CHANNEL, MOVE ENERGY, AND DROP THE STORIES FOR PRESENCE AND EMPOWERMENT

One day while I was using plant medicine, I was deeply connecting with myself in meditation, and I realized that we carry so many stories—stories and beliefs about everything. Some are empowering based on experiences and some disempowering, some made up, some given to us. So many, many stories. These thoughts and beliefs and stories create everything. I heard deep down that I need to drop the stories, at least the disempowering ones. Often, I do my best to drop all stories and just find myself shifting into the belief that anything is possible because who knows, and I keep it open. I feel my power rise up when I find myself letting go of all the stories and creating from a blank slate. I use this belief to see things from different vantage points, which is awareness and power. When we are tied to stories, we are stuck, stuck with how things will play out. We are stuck with stories and patterns in our energetic fields, and we witness them play out in our reality. Often when I feel stressed out or triggered or would think something is happening, I would say to myself, "Drop all the stories. Stop right now and take a breath and drop this story. Empty your channel and just be for a moment." In doing this in the moment, you move from being the participant to the watcher, and when you back up and take a minute, you move yourself and your energy, and you can feel/see differently. We shift from the mind to the heart. This is truth and this is power. We have all created our own storms and gotten pulled into other people's storms, but this is holding space for yourself.

I remember the first time I was in a conversation with my partner that was becoming emotionally charged. Emotions were becoming charged, and I was able to drop the story and breathe and just listen while watching and feeling instead of letting myself be pulled into the storm.

At that moment, I was able to hold space for my partner and myself without judgment, and I felt so calm and clear-minded. Our stories and attachments can be a good thing because they show us where we are struggling to let go, and they can teach us how to surrender in the moment and how to consciously hold space for ourselves and others, and move energy. When my channel is open and clear, I can feel and be pure awareness and just simply watch and trust, which is power.

Before I realized this, my channel felt peaceful and sort of empty after I would dance, exercise, meditate but really, I give myself permission now to empty my channel and feel peace and simply watch. It's interesting because once you start to embody some of these things and you go back and speak with others, you can see how exhausting it was for you and how exhausting it is for others. How we hold on so deeply to how we feel when really, it's all just moving, and the struggle is exhausting. Now yes, struggle is part of the path but at some point, don't you want to do something different, create different, feel different? We are so much more than we will ever know, and these small things turn into massive shifts.

I often remember to drop the stories and to be pure awareness when I deeply connect with myself in the morning and at night. When I feel triggered or when I am struggling, I remind myself to come back to my sacred space and show my true face by watching and just being. When was the last time you dropped all the stories to simply watch and be? Try it and see how you feel. All of the energy about not trusting and worrying and going round and round is conserved for pouring more love into you and for enjoyment and for channeling your power. We give so much power away by tying ourselves to these stories that simply create more lack, confusion, and paralysis. There is so much power in our choices. What will you choose?

A FEW IMPORTANT THINGS THAT WILL BEGIN TO SHIFT YOUR MIND, ENERGY, AND REALITY

The most important thing I think we will ever realize is that being present and being aligned is all the power we need. It starts with healing, dropping the stories, and showing up as we are with an open heart and an open mind and understanding and learning to embody empowerment through mentalism and energetic tools. We are already everything, and we are already ready regardless of how it feels or the stories we find ourselves attached to that are holding us back. At least this is the most important thing I have ever realized, and from that moment on, I felt I could trust my life, myself, and begin to love myself more by honoring myself consistently no matter where I am on my path. All of this creates presence and the ability to be in the moment. All of this creates a peace within that you don't have to chase but simply erase the obstacles. All of this creates a path for your power to flow through you and help you master yourself and all the things life will throw at you.

Chapter 11

THE TOOLS THAT CHANGE EVERYTHING

SOME OF MY FAVORITE HEALING TOOLS

My favorite tools for healing are floating, EFT, meditation, Solfeggio Frequencies, essential oils, sound healing, Reiki, and psychedelics. I will discuss some of these below.

When we arrive here on earth, we don't get a manual, and we don't always know what we are looking for as far as tools that can help us to heal and expand in love. We all come here to overcome different things, but one thing is for sure we are here to remember who we are and to share our gifts with the world. Before we can begin, we need to heal so we can find our balance and be in flow.

Float Tank/Sensory Deprivation

My first experience with the float tank was magical beyond words. I first heard about it on Joe Rogan's podcast, as my friend and I used to listen to his podcasts all the time. I decided to do it because I was scared to be enclosed and thought that I was getting to the point where I was sick of fear driving my decisions. So what. I was claustrophobic. I started to get to the point where I was sick of wondering who I really was and what I could do if fear stopped suffocating me all the time. So I booked my first float, and I remember feeling scared and knowing that everything I wanted was on the other side, so I just started doing things that I was afraid of. As I stepped into the tank, I felt excited but a little like, okay, here we go.

This is what I wrote after my first experience with sensory deprivation: The English language is so limited to try and explain something so that was so life changing for the better.

It was pitch black. I could see nothing and hear nothing. I have never felt so relaxed and held by the universe, but so conscious I felt such a deep level of peace and awareness. It was like liquid love. I was just floating hand over head and just... There aren't even words to explain what it was like. It was like I was within and without. I started asking my guides and higher self questions, and then I started hearing all the answers. Not much different from waking life, but it felt so much more intense. It felt like the work you would do over ten meditations was being done in one hour. It was incredibly accelerated. I have been that deep within meditation where you don't feel you have a body but not to that level.

After I had no more things to contemplate at that time in between being present and silent, I felt an overwhelming feeling of self-love for myself. I kept smiling. It felt like the illusions of 3-D always had kind of stopped the flow of love for myself. I felt like I was pure consciousness. I had no idea how much time went by in there. It felt like I always was and would always be, and that time truly was not real. I have never felt so relaxed and charged up.

I did feel very vulnerable and thought that if you are not used to being comfortable within your mind, it could be very scary if you do not meditate. If you are a slave to your mind, this could feel like hell, hence the reason some have panic attacks in there. I remember feeling incredibly vulnerable like I could choose to get upset and scared or embrace it in love, and I chose love. I remember just grabbing myself and holding my breasts and saying I love myself. It was as if I had a first glimpse of myself, as if I had been avoiding that moment for some time, and it was beyond magical.

After the first time, I was obsessed. I remember going home and feeling ecstasy and closing my eyes and just feeling absolute peace and love, and I slept so well that night. It was as if I was able to bring my vibrational alignment higher than it had ever been by seeing pieces of me that I had never seen before.

Since that first time, there have been so many other times, and each time has been more magical than the last. I would start to go in with a plan to release, to drop in deep, and forgive myself and others, and let it go. I would call my energy back, cut cords, and feel into the experience. The third time I went in, I was asking for guidance, and I heard, "You know what to do." A close friend of mine, Denise, an intuitive energy healing practitioner, called me and told me a few hours later "I had a dream, and the guidance was, 'You know what to do.'" It was true. I was at the point where I did know what to do.

I had another time I went into the float tank with my close friend and private yoga teacher Kevin Oroszlan. I was in the tank, and he was in the tank next to me. As someone who is clairaudient, I remember hearing laughing in my head and thinking, "That is so strange." When we got out, and we discussed his experience, he said that he had a hard time dropping in at first, and then he started laughing like a madman, and I thought, "Oh, okay, that was what that was." I have had so many amazing and healing experiences in the tank over and over. I always come out with new insights and feeling peaceful and more awake and aware and giddy with a big smile on my face. I always sleep so deep and feel amazing. The float tank is an amazing tool for transcending illusions.

EFT

EFT is an emotional freedom technique made famous by Nick Ortner. It is tapping energy meridians in conjunction with saying a positive mantra. So essentially, it is a psychological acupressure technique. This helps release negative emotions stored in the body. I have been using this technique for many years when I felt nervous before making videos for my Facebook Live and my YouTube channel. I also have used it when I was incredibly sad and crying during a big release when I was purging.

I remember when I had to tell my parents that I was going to write about my past sexual abuse and I was so sick. I felt ill, so worried that my parents would not love me anymore and would not be proud of me and would think so much less of me. I messaged them both, and I remember standing in the bathroom, wondering when I would speak to them, and I was crying to the point of almost throwing up. I don't know that I have ever felt that awful, well, awful isn't even the right word. It was such a deep fear and disgust for the situation, but I knew if I didn't dive into that terrible moment and tell my truth, I would be agreeing to suffocate for the rest of my life, and it had already been decades that I was living with that secret.

Secrets are so heavy, and they weigh us down to a point we don't realize, stopping us from ever taking flight. So in that moment of processing that darkness, I used tapping to calm down and release what I was feeling. Within a minute, I was past the point of hysterically crying and wanting to throw up. EFT is an amazing tool that can help us release, and that is the key to not getting sick. Sickness so often happens when we suppress and hold emotions within our bodies.

Meditation

Meditation started for me about fifteen years ago when I lost my job in Brooklyn. Most of us understand and know the power of committing to a regular practice. It is by far the best thing I have ever committed to in my life. For all of the contemplation and seeking within the silence of my soul, nothing could have brought me to this moment where I am now.

When I lost my job, I remember seeing a Deepak and Oprah meditation challenge for one month, and I thought, "Wow, that looks fun!" But I wasn't sure how to even be silent, let alone enjoy the silence. I was very type-A at that point, always in a rush. I lived in New Jersey and spent a lot of time in New York City, and rushing was as normal as the air I was breathing. Doing something all the time was normal. I was always pushing to see how much more I could do because my external validation was everything to me. It was who I was. My identity. Achievement was everything.

I had no idea who I was or what I was doing and what I wanted. I was running like a hamster on a wheel. Just go, go, go. I remember losing my job and feeling so sad and anxious about my future. But then a few days after I started spending time at the park, and without all the daily distractions, I started to hear my soul whispering to me. I started meditating. The first time felt so strange. I remember thinking, "Am I even doing this right? Was it supposed to be like that?" I kept up with it, and I started to see images and colors and hear more guidance. I started to feel so much inner peace that I had never felt. I also started to get more and more guidance that was louder than ever before, and with

this new channel opened, I felt things deeper than I had ever felt. Everything was shifting.

Within a few months, I discovered the Omvana app by Mindvalley and started using neuro-linguistic programming (NLP) and binaural beats, and then my expansion really took off. NLP is hypnosis, and it is incredibly powerful. A lot of our decisions and thought patterns originate in our unconscious mind, and so it directs a big part of our experience and our holographic reality. So when I started to see things I was struggling with in my life reflected back to me about my inner world, I would use NLP. I would wake up and feel like a minor tweak had taken place, and things began to shift little by little. NLP and binaural beats are amazing tools for shifting, healing, and awareness.

Essential oils

Essential oils have quite literally changed my life. Most of you probably already know that they are amazing tools to help us stay in balance, or get in balance when we get thrown out. Scent is incredibly powerful. The first recorded uses of essential oils were back in 2697 and 2597 BCE. Aromatherapy is a form of alternative medicine in which essential oils are used to affect a person's mind, body, mood, or cognitive function. Some essential oils act as adaptogens, which are natural balancers. It is said that professional practitioners use approximately 300 essential oils to treat a range of illnesses, and shamans have possessed an understanding of the healing power of plants for thousands of years. Aromatherapy is an incredibly powerful tool for finding or maintaining daily balance. Where we find our balance is where we find our way. Many people find that aromatherapy helps to create balance within, and promote a stronger mind-body-spirit connection. My passion for aromatherapy led me to create my new spelled oil line Hermetic Spell after mixing custom oils for sound healing and reiki sessions for a few years for my clients.

Music moves

Music is magic. It truly is, and magic moves. Music moves our soul. When we feel broken, bruised, and beaten, music can speak for us, lulling us back into balance. I have music playing all the time, especially when I am going through a stressful time. You know when you are in the car, and maybe you feel a little low, and your jam comes on? Hell, yeah! Then all of a sudden, you are singing along and feeling good. Music heals us. There is even sound therapy that helps balance our mind, body, and spirit back into alignment.

So there are two different areas I use music for in my life. There are the shows I am passionate about. My passion is for trance, hardstyle, hardcore, and DNB. This is the music that is on daily that elevates my vibration as I melt into the soundwaves and stay fluid in my flow. I go to as many shows as I can on the weekends. Really all music that you love is going to heal. They say that when you are happy, you feel the music, and when you are sad, you feel the lyrics even more. I think we hear and feel no matter how we feel.

The second type of music is the music I consciously use for healing at night when I am resting, meditating, or sleeping. The music I love for healing while at rest is the Solfeggio frequencies and sound healing with Tibetan bowls. Anytime we are working through negative emotions that lower our vibrational frequency and we feel out of balance, these three types of music can help lift our vibration back up. It's just knowing when to use what.

Solfeggio Frequencies

Solfeggio frequencies were sound frequencies used in Gregorian chants.

Dr. Joseph Puleo, a naturopathic physician, researched the Solfeggio frequencies back in the 1970s. In his examination of the Bible, he found in certain chapters and verses, a pattern of six repeating codes around a series of sacred numbers, 3, 6, and 9. We all remember Nikola Tesla said, "If you only knew the magnificence of the 3, 6 and 9, then you would have a key to the universe." When Dr. Joseph Puleo deciphered these using the ancient Pythagorean method of reducing the verse numbers to their single digit integers, the codes revealed a series of six electromagnetic sound frequencies that correspond to the six missing tones of the ancient Solfeggio scale.

The Solfeggio frequencies contain the six pure tonal notes that were once used to make up the ancient musical scale, until, it has been presumed, they were altered by the Catholic Church and Pope Gregory I (better known as "Gregory the Great"), who served from 590 to 604 AD.

These are the Solfeggio frequencies:

UT – 396 Hz – Liberating Guilt and Fear

RE – 417 Hz – Undoing Situations and Facilitating Change

MI – 528 Hz – Transformation and Miracles (DNA Repair - Repair - and derives from the phrase "*MI-ra-gestorum*" in Latin meaning "miracle.")

FA – 639 Hz – Connecting/Relationships

SOL – 741 Hz – Awakening Intuition

LA – 852 Hz – Returning to Spiritual Order

Sound is a vibration, and everything vibrates, and everything is energy.

Chapter 12

MY TOOLS AND EXPERIENCE

The tools I have been using in my private practice that I specialized in is the power of three because then we can see. I use sound healing in conjunction with Reiki and custom oil alchemy.

Over the years, I have witnessed so much growth, expansion, healing, and open-hearted-ness, and self-realization from my clients, it's the reason why I chose to come here to help.

I want to see you win, but we have to begin to invest in ourselves. The biggest lesson I learned while using energy tools and from the coaches I have worked with is that when we are scared we need to invest in ourselves, we are not able to fully receive because we don't believe we are worthy. For me, I spent thousands of dollars on my partners in relationships but then when it would come to investing in me or my business, this was a huge block, and I was stuck for a long time. When I began to use energy tools, everything changed.

To heal is to call your power back. To find your balance is to find harmony within, and when the two come together, we become inspired to create with magic.

To be in balance is to embody the beauty of who you truly are. To respect, honor, and embrace your inner rhythm, to understand how to flow and to go and to grow. To not feel guilty about being and about doing and knowing which one to do when. Balance is harmony, and it is so overlooked, but if you look within, you will hear and feel what you need, and no one can tell you what that is. I hope that you have the courage to honor your inner rhythm and move with love and awareness for you. Consider daily what balance means to you.

There is a time to speak and a time to be quiet. A time to be bound and a time to be found. A time to go dark and a time to light a spark. Start a fire. Your mind is a fucking liar. Burn, baby, burn, won't you ever learn? Resist, and it will persist. The dark and the light is the fight, neither one is right, but do delight, with all your might, with sound and sight.

Balance: By definition, balance is mental steadiness or emotional stability; habit of calm behavior, judgment, etc.

What does balance mean to you, right here, right now?

Balance: To be in balance is to embody the beauty of who you truly are. To respect, honor, and embrace your inner rhythm, to understand how to flow and to go and to grow and to know what you need when you need it. To not feel guilty about being and about doing and knowing which one to do when. Balance is harmony, and it is so overlooked, but if you look within, you will hear and feel what you need, and no one can tell you what that is. I hope that you have the courage to honor your inner rhythm and move with love and awareness for you. Consider daily what balance means to you. Balance is the balance of masculine and feminine energy. It is the balance and alignment of mind, body, and spirit. When we are in balance, all things are possible, and there is no struggle. We are in a state of flow.

As we find ourselves on a lifelong healing journey, the next important piece of being in flow is balance. There is no way to be in an optimal state of flow if you are out of balance. Everything within us and out in the world is interconnected, and when we know this, we realize the utmost importance of being in balance. We make no apologies for turning inward, phones off, for taking deep breaths, and for taking time to honor, love, and respect not only ourselves but our path. Whatever we need, we make no apologies as we know we have to come first so that we can go out into the world centered to do amazing things. We have contemplated daily what balance means to us and how to embody it, along with honoring the ever-changing and constant healing process. The thing about balance is that it is changing every second of every day. Some days we need a break, and some days we are in an optimal state of flow where we can do and do and do. Being aware enough to know what we truly need is incredibly important. Sometimes balance is just a small movement here or there, or it's a massive shift away in a totally different direction, but only you know in your heart of hearts what you need and when you need it.

I used to follow the rules and do what they told me to do, and I was so out of balance.

For the longest time, I used to follow the rules. I went on chasing after what they told me to want. Men, cars, marriage, things, to be a better version of me out of fear, not out of love. I wanted to be what they told me to be. I wanted all the things to fill me up, but at some point, I realized relying on external things was a recipe for disaster. I wanted to have what they told me to want. I wanted to fit in, and I did what was expected. I was terrified to be me and to stand out, and then slowly—I don't even know when it quite happened, but it started shifted—I started shifting. My ideas about who I was and what

I wanted felt like an out of date outfit, like nothing fit me anymore. It felt like I was suffocating because my life no longer worked for me.

This isn't about what is right or wrong because there is no such thing as right or wrong, but there is such a thing as right or wrong for you and for me. That is the question, and that is the one we should be tapping into daily for aligning with who we truly are, and moving closer to what we want and how we want to feel. We are the creators of our experience distilled through our thoughts, beliefs, actions, words, and energy, and if our programming is built on what they told you, then I am afraid you won't feel quite like you, but more like when Alice says, "Who in the world am I? Ah, that's the great puzzle."

Something happens when we break rules and live from our heart space.

It started after years of working in the corporate world, where you had to separate the real from the fake, and there was most often a lot at stake. The world of surface connections and stress and office politics that can often make you sick from the outside in. It started to happen when I realized that I was slaving away at a place that didn't care about me, and that was crushing my spirit one day at a time. Mentally, emotionally, and physically, this place was making me sick, so sick. My other co-workers felt the same. The mental abuse and the unprofessionalism and the illegal stuff that went on, I was absolutely fucking horrified.

As time went on, it was blatantly obvious that I was never going to find balance and happiness within in a toxic environment. This statement seems so obvious now, but back then, I believed that this was the only way. As a very honest and authentic person, every time we were asked to hire people, I struggled because I wouldn't wish that job on anyone. I was so incredibly grateful for that job and the experience. It showed me what not to do and what not to invest myself in. I started to realize that balance growth and freedom belonged to the entrepreneur or to the place where you are valued. Not everyone is going to go out on their own, and sometimes it isn't forever, but there are great teams, and there are bad teams. After what I had experienced and as scared as I was about going out on my own, I was more scared to invest my future into this crazy out-of-balance place, and so it was time to choose me.

I was very scared, but I honestly had just had enough. It was time to go out on my own for a while and explore. So I broke the old rules about how you build your career, and I built my own business. Choosing someone else at that time was scary. Choosing me was awesome! I knew that there would be things that I didn't know, but I could figure it out, and I could ask for help. That I would, in fact, figure it out. That I would learn a lot about myself going out on my own into waters I had never surfed before. My parents raised me to work hard and to believe that I could go anywhere and do anything. I believed them, and so I did. Sometimes things can be simple if you just dive in. Even if you didn't have a support system that lifted you and guided you, it is never too late to start shifting your old beliefs and instill new ones that support you on your journey up and over to the next level of love and above.

One of the most and pressing questions I ask myself every week is, who would we be if we were free? This helps me see what is holding me back and what patterns I have been just existing through

SIMPLE, QUICK AND PRACTICAL PRACTICES FOR SHIFTING INTO EMPOWERMENT AND ALIGNMENT WITH SOURCE IN THE MOMENT

Often, we can spend most of our time feeling very overwhelmed and not sure where to start. Often things are way too complicated, and I am one who can be very lazy. I used to joke that I was royalty in a past life because there are times in my life when I have felt so lazy and struggle to stay committed. Although once I began connecting to myself, I knew and felt that alignment is the most powerful vibrational alignment and state you can exist in where all is possible. What I have realized over the years of building sacred space and staying connected to me and aligned, the practices are the same. The truth is, there are no wrong moves because no matter how much you have neglected yourself in the past or not forgiven yourself and others, you are always making your way to where you are going. Sometimes it may take a little longer.

Ultimately sacred space and staying connected to your inner being and source is a choice and a moment in which you give yourself permission, and you dedicate your energy awareness and love to yourself first and then to others. What happens over time when you begin to practice these simple but powerful things—your love, awareness, gratitude, and presence—you find a state of mind and energetic state that really you can't be fucked with. You decided those silly things that bother people no longer affect you. You have a halo of love around you in this space, you feel free to honor your light, and you're dark. Free to say I love you; you are beautiful and free to set a boundary and tell someone to fuck off. Self-love and boundaries are one and the same. You feel no shame in your authenticity and the embodiment of who you truly are as your spirit dances day by day.

If you want to be free, you have to decide, and then you have to reinforce this decision by being congruent with your thoughts, beliefs, actions, and vibrational frequency. True power is finding the balance in being grounded in your 3-D experience and also being connected to the spirit world, for we experience both whether or not we are aware of it.

PRACTICES TO STAY CONNECTED TO YOURSELF NO MATTER WHERE YOU ARE OR WHAT IS HAPPENING

Breathe* Never underestimate the power of your breath. When I was sexually abused, I spent many years not breathing properly as my anxiety reached insane levels where I wanted to jump out of my body. I did not feel safe or at home in my sacred vessel. I didn't feel safe to breathe or be seen. Just that alone gave me an insane amount of anxiety, especially in public. On top of not feeling grounded in my experience, or feeling safe having gifts and being able to feel others, added to a very uncomfortable time when I had to be out in public. It was pretty much torture. I hated eye contact, and I hated feeling others as I did not even feel comfortable in my own body and mind. I believe most live this way. A lot of people who have anxiety are sometimes feeling others. It is important to realize that everything we feel is not ours energetically.

You know that feeling when you are having a great day, then someone who is angry comes into the room, and your stomach hurts, and you feel sick? Yes, that's you feeling that person. I have been walking down the street and had what appeared to be a homeless woman who was ranting loudly, and I immediately felt anxious. When she yelled at me, I felt a shock go through my body. Many of us are very sensitive to energy. Focusing on breath work is a powerful way to reconnect in seconds. Get into the mindset that the state of your breathing is important and be conscious of whether or not you are breathing shallow or deep. Whatever your mental state call attention to your breath. A simple in for three out for four can connect you to yourself and ground you. Air, energy, emotions—it all needs to move. Often your breath will mirror your state of mind, so actively controlling your breath is powerful. Breathing properly can instantly help to make you feel relaxed, give you more energy, and reduce anxiety and depression. Do not underestimate the power of something so simple as consciously breathing.

A hand on your heart and an acknowledgment of self in this moment, Ilearned that one of the statements you always make is that you deeply love and accept yourself. I deeply love and accept myself. Feel the power behind that statement. Can you feel it? It resonates on an incredibly high and pure vibrational frequency, which transforms. EFT (emotional freedom technique) essentially helps you be present in the moment and release stress and emotional problems. When using EFT, you are tapping near endpoints of "energy meridians" to reduce tension and promote a stronger mind-body connection. The statements made as you tap these points are speaking to your subconscious mind. It is an incredibly powerful practice in being present. Every time I used it, whether I was crying, or felt stuck on something in my mind and felt very anxious as I was struggling with letting go, it helped me to transform my energy instantly and calm my mind. Even if there wasn't relief to the point that I wanted, I was acknowledging myself in that moment and loving myself exactly as I am. Loving yourself in any moment exactly as you are—crying on the floor, broken, suicidal, whatever or wherever you are—is the most powerful thing you can and will ever do. Self-love and self-acknowledgment are the most powerful things you can and will ever do. When you have begun to choose you, you can then begin to hold space for others in a most magical way because you understand how to hold yourself and others with unconditional love.

The statement, I deeply love and accept myself, is incredibly powerful and connects you instantly to your heart and your truth and puts you back in your body to feel, instead of living in your mind out of the present moment. Anxiety and resistance cannot live in the present moment. Fear and worry cannot live in the present moment when you surrender. This statement, this declaration, is a declaration of permission, love, power, and truth. I truly believe that every single thought and action is either choosing and declaring, "I love myself, and I want to be empowered, and I accept myself," or "I am rejecting myself, I am disempowered, and I am struggling to love myself." Our words are spells and magic which manifest whether or not you have realized, accepted, and engaged consciously or unconsciously. Our words, feelings, and actions are the fabric of our reality that we create and how we raise or lower our vibrational frequency consciously or unconsciously.

I noticed one day during meditation a few years in, that I received some guidance and realization that we ignore ourselves constantly, that I had been ignoring myself for a long time in many ways, and it was contributing to limiting patterns, stuck energy, and confusion, and being ungrounded and unfocused. Have you noticed that about yourself? We quite often and constantly ignore ourselves, reinforcing the fact that we do not honor, respect, or love ourselves, and we wonder why others don't as well. We wonder why others don't treat us well. Are you treating yourself well? There is no faking energy. It is always felt on a conscious or subconscious level. We work when we don't feel well; we rush around, ignoring our basic needs. We feel guilt or shame when our body wants pleasure. We don't feel deserving of basic needs such as sleep, pleasure, food, and whatever else we need. We put others' needs in front of our own because we live from a fear of not being enough. We don't take the time to look at what we have been through and heal because we are scared to face who we are and what has happened to us.

I noticed as a survivor of abuse, for years, I had so much resistance to receiving. I even had resistance around feeling like I deserved to feel good. I used to force myself to work out when I felt shitty. I was always pushing myself because I didn't feel worthy in the past. So sad and so disrespectful. I lived as a victim for a long time as if things were just happening to me. The stories I told myself were very disempowering until I started to realize most of what I believed about the fabric of my reality was based in limiting illusions. When I began to find my truth, my power began to rise up.

When we love ourselves, we meet our basic needs. We rely on ourselves to be happy, not on anyone else or any circumstances. We don't empower other people to disrupt our world by placing expectations on others. We are attached to nothing; we don't need anything to be a certain way as we are deeply connected to and in love with ourselves. When we love ourselves, we are balanced. When we love ourselves, we feel safe to be in the moment. Being present and simply honoring yourself is the beginning process of moving forward. When you love yourself, you are invested and interested in healing and embodying peace. You begin to feel turned off by people and situations that no longer resonate. You start to honor yourself, and you stop settling.

As I meditated and looked closer over the years, there was always more to see. This was a big one.

Your soul wants you to know your truth. Your spirit wants you to embody your truth. Your spirit craves alignment and connection with your inner being and source. When you decide to face you and to be true in the view, you will be held in love and pure awareness, you are always safe to see and be who you are, and this will take you far. The first step to healing is being present and grounding into this moment and to acknowledge yourself. Stop ignoring you, stop running from who you are, and stop ignoring your needs. You need to feed mind, body, and spirit. I know that you hear it.

Consciously talk to yourself every day* Whether you realize it or not, your body and your cells hear you every single day—your thoughts, your beliefs, and your stories. This controls your vibrational frequency and how your reality manifests and the experiences that come to you. I read online that you should make a recording of what you want and of things you are working on and let it play every single night before you go to sleep. I began doing this months ago, and I wanted to see how fast things change. I went from a place of wanting to a place of watching everything just happen incredibly fast. I have always been one of those people who talk to themselves, probably because I am incredibly creative, and I am always channeling a ton of information on the daily. Every morning I take a minute to set my intention for the day and talk to myself. I like to call it my daily permission and prayer of surrender. I deeply love and accept myself, and no matter what happens today, I am in control of me, where my attention goes and flows. I love my body, and I love how I am; I will do my best to be present and open in love. I keep my channel clear of the stories because I am not limited. Anything is possible because I am a powerful and infinite being. When I had cancer at eighteen and beat it in eight months, I know most of it was my mind. I watched fear with curiosity and didn't much engage with it. I knew even back then about energy conservation, as I would simply watch. I didn't allow it to take me under. I would talk to my body and lay my hands over my body in love and focus. This was years before I learned Reiki. I was intuitively just talking to my body. Eight months later, I was free from cancer, and that was twenty-three years ago. Your words are powerful. Choose them wisely and in love.

Dance* I remember being chased by boys on the playground. I remember being so fast. I remember the freedom in movement, and I remember when that seemed like it was gone, the sadness and the restriction. I remember the first time men started to stare at me. I remember the first time I felt ashamed of being naked. This infinite, magical, amazing soul in this weird little human body, so weird and funny this human experience. I remember getting older as my body developed and missing the absence of my breasts because I loved to run fast, and I felt free, and then just like that, I had this body that took up space. I resisted my body for a long time. It is so funny.

Most of us want what we don't have, but as we begin to surrender to what we are, we become the most beautiful. We blossom and bloom and make some room. For the longest time, I felt uncomfortable dancing, and that freedom felt gone from my life. I had no idea what a big deal having big breasts was going to be like. For years I hid under Brooks Brothers shirts, but my boobs didn't like that, and they were always busting the buttons open at the most awkward times. Hiding my body didn't keep me safe from being molested as a child or raped in college.

It's a strange experience to be a person but have people be obsessed with your avatar, this physical body that you are living in in this incarnation, as if your mind doesn't exist and you don't have anything to say. It's weird to see women jealous and angry because of a physical attribute, and try and body shame you like you should cover up. As I healed from the trauma that happened to me, the way people react and project no longer affects me. I find it interesting, and then I look away should the behavior not come from a place of love and respect.

I remember the days of self-loathing and forcing myself not to eat and work out a lot. There was a lot of time I spent forgiving myself and others and healing my body. These days I notice I am no longer suffocating. Do you feel like you can't dance freely or even move freely? Now I prioritize movement and pleasure above all else, and respect and love and honor my body moment by moment. Any time you feel upset or stuck, just start moving. Sometimes I even move while I meditate with my eyes closed. It's as if I am more connected to my body and its need to move. Dance is healing and helps the energy move, and energy needs to move freely at all times, or we get stuck. My friend Rachel used to say give yourself permission to dance, and yet I would freeze and feel strange in my sacred vessel until I stopped judging myself and started moving. Working out or dancing can shift you instantly, so I hope you dance daily.

Make art and/or express yourself* So often, we don't feel safe to communicate our needs or express them. I continued to hear guidance and channeled messages for years before I decided to begin my book and online class. I began to notice I didn't feel connected to the real me when I wasn't able to create or express even through short video messages. Years later, there isn't a day that goes by that I don't write or dance or create something for me or to help others. I know I used to be scared because I didn't feel free or safe, and I worried, "Are people going to think I am weird? Do people even understand me?" My ego was incredibly loud and was trying to stop me from living and embodying my true self. As time went on, I kept connecting deeply to me and my path through sound healing sessions on myself, Reiki, meditation, and plant medicine. I kept seeking my truth. I stopped taking classes and reading other people's stuff; I just kept diving deep and going within. It happened slowly but expressing and making art is both healing and empowering. When was the last time you made art or felt unrestrained and were able to express yourself freely in love and channel your pure awareness out into the ether? What are you waiting for? There will never be another you, and you have gifts to share with the world, so please don't delay.

The most important thing I have learned to stay connected to myself and balance and clear energy is a morning Reiki session. There have been many times in my life my energy has been all messed up, and it wasn't always from my stuff. It was from being out in the world and interacting with others. When I began doing Kundalini, a lot of stories came up for me to clear, but then there would be days I felt peaceful and happy, and I was radiating. Money was flowing.

Why creative visualization is overlooked and how it can cause instant miracles and faster manifestations when you consciously feel and are more present.

Creative visualization with your eyes closed and open* As children, we use creative visualization constantly. We are tapped in in a very powerful way. As we get older, we tend not to use creative visualization for fun and manifesting but to replay stories and scenarios that disempower us, create anxiety, and ultimately push us into lowering our vibration and sometimes even depression or suicidal tendencies. Intuitively we know when to use visualization. When I got cancer at eighteen and beat it in eight months, it was because I knew what needed to be done.

Most talk about creating and closing your eyes and visualizing, but you can also do this with your eyes open. You are constantly manifesting every second of every day, so why not make a conscious effort to use visualization as often as you can. I especially love to play this game when I am moving through my day. I first thought about it when Abraham Hicks said that you should play a game called ignore reality. I use situations when I used to feel most stressed to move energy and create.

For instance, I love to play this in traffic, and in LA, there is always traffic it seems. Instead of feeling resistant to the traffic, I use my mind to connect to all the cars around me, and I sync into them and change the energy to feel as though the cars are moving with me and I create an intention and want, a desire. I feel and imagine all of the cars as energy that is moving toward my cause and desire as I can feel and imagine it being manifested faster. Eventually, the traffic takes off and moves, and then I know/feel that my desire is on the way.

You can do anything you want with your imagination. I love to use visualization when I am doing Kundalini kriyas, imagining that my aura is healthy, strong, and can extend very far distances at will. Even on walks, you can imagine that as you walk, you are getting closer to your desire and leaving things that no longer resonate behind. You can imagine yourself at the ocean as you become a drop of water and merge back into the ocean and harness the entire ocean to power up and help you manifest faster or connect with the earth to fill your channel back up with energy. Imagination can be used to heal, get more energy, manifest, and change your mental, emotional, and energetic states.

When I first started meditating two decades ago, I didn't feel as though my imagination was that strong. Still, as I meditated and began practicing creating and destroying in my mind, I got stronger, and so will you. This came in handy when I began doing Reiki/sound healings. I was able to draw symbols, feel and see colors and use them and clear, while also holding and grounding my clients in love as they heal and become more aligned. Visualization is fun and powerful, so use it as often as you feel called to it. You will begin to get so good it won't matter if you do it with your eyes closed or open. All is mental.

With every decision, we either empower ourselves or disempower ourselves. With our awareness, we must choose wisely. I began to choose me; fear was over my shoulder every step of the way, but I kept moving closer to who I truly was and what I truly wanted, and it felt hella good.

Heal yourself

Face your fears head-on

Once you realize that it is time to face your fears and that it has never really been about the right time, you will realize there is no time when everything feels right to do something, but we must dive in. We are victims of our own mind. The truth is, we will never feel ready, but despite that, it is always the right time to begin. There is no such thing as feeling ready. When it arrives, the door is here. It just appears, and we walk near, leave the fear, and walk through. Right here, right now, just trust you, trust spirit, trust in divine timing and dive in and begin!

Mantra: I am connected to the light from above and below. I am one with spirit. The universe fully supports me. I trust me, and I trust my path. It's not a matter of if, but when. All things are flowing to me now. I trust.

What are you still scared of? What would you do if fear were not staring back at you?

Heal yourself

The wave of confusion

When we feel we are struggling and or hurting, ask yourself, is it a pain that you have been holding onto, or is it your mind that is spinning you out, or is it a real thing that you need to feel? Is it real? Are you upset because your beliefs do not support you on your journey? Are you truly upset and need to feel this pain to release it? Understand why you feel a certain way, and if the way you feel is based on something real or an illusion.

For instance, if someone you love dies, this is real, and it would be natural for you to feel sadness and anger and many other emotions. If you have expectations for the way you want something to happen, but it didn't. Those emotions are a choice you are making when you could easily let go and accept what is. We decide everything, even whether or not to react to our emotions, which are just passing through.

There are many decisions and vantage points and different vibrational frequencies and narratives we can choose from which we can operate from within. The only way to move through the madness is to have the awareness to act from your soul and not from the madness in your mind. Our mind is a mental prison, and the invisible constraints we have been imposing on ourselves can cause so many imagined problems. The question to ask yourself is, can you tell the difference between what your mind has been programmed to want and think and what you as a soul want and know? Are you upset because you have ideas about the way things should be or the way you should be? So many things can be released by simply walking through the whys of what you feel and think. They can also be released by meditating to a higher state of consciousness, which causes your mind to be blank, present, and peaceful more often. There are many ways to elevate past.

There are the daily distractions that upset most of us, but we can dive deep and shift those beliefs so we can be and feel more peaceful. There are very real things that can disrupt our peace, such as losing someone we care about or being in a tough place in life where everything feels like a challenge. Other than that, most of the stuff we find ourselves engrossed and upset with in the day-to-day living is not that important. As Mooji says, "It's nothing; it's nothing, it's nothing." It truly is nothing. What we give power to, we give power over us. It's your decision, and it always will be. You choose. We have to go within and have a serious higher self soul conversation about what is important and why and what do we need to reevaluate and let go of.

There will come a time where you no longer seek outside guidance but fully trust your intuition and your oneness with the universe. You will understand what is in your heart and what is not aligned with you. Family and friends will begin to fall out of your holographic reality, and there will be some push back, and some will distance themselves from you but continue to speak your truth from your heart space with love and respect for yourself and other souls that you interact with. Keep moving forward on your path. Other souls that are on the same vibrational frequency will come closer. This happened to me when I moved to LA. I started to meet my soul family, my spiritual friends, and my rave family, and it was most magical. I started to have some of the most amazing friendships I have ever had, soul connections that lifted me in love.

So have you decided to get onto your surfboard, or are you drowning in the sea barely breathing?

Heal yourself
Learning all the lessons

Have you learned the lessons only of those who admired you, and were tender with you, and stood aside for you? Have you not learned great lessons from those who braced themselves against you, and disputed passage with you? - Walt Whitman

We are here for a reason. We all have gifts to share with the world. We have lessons to learn. It is our soul's calling to share those lessons and gifts with the world to inspire ourselves and others. To continuously heal ourselves and to help others heal. To share our experience with the world, and to speak our authentic voices. To inspire others to stand up and speak their authentic truths. There are so many lessons in all of our experiences and so much potential for growth from within. There is something so amazing and wondrous about the dance of life. The act of living and figuring things out, to being present and eventually living our soul's calling. To work out these lessons day in and day out and to build something that is special to us. To create. To breathe and love and live. Surely there are many mysteries we shall never know in just this lifetime, but oh, there are some things that we will live, learn, and share, and that is the gift of our experience. I have experienced some very dark things in my life, and they helped me grow if not more than some of my lightest and happiest moments. For we learn how to maneuver through these tragic things that eventually breathe strength and power into us if we decide that we want to draw that from them. We can always choose to be a victim or a victor. I choose to be a victor for all my days in all ways.

Are you a victor or a victim? Make your choice. Do you feel powerful yet?

Do you trust your experience yet? It has led you here. Are you ready to run towards you in every view and stay true?

The fear I feel.

The worry I feel.

The anxiety I feel.

The hurt I feel.

The pain I feel.

The attachment I have.

The ideas I have about how things should be versus the current and actual reality.

The separation I am creating.

Right here, right now, I release all of these. I release all that no longer serves me.

Open your heart, breathe into your heart space, and connect to the light from above and below and sit in silence, deeply dive into the silence of your soul. The light and love showering you from above and below. Feel your guides and angels lifting you, protecting you, carrying you. You are love and trust and peace underneath all the noise of your mind. In silence is where we feel it and see it without sight and sound. It's where we are found and no longer bound, so stick around.

What's *for* me won't miss me. I've learned that I choose my narrative because I create and manifest from how I see this view. I have learned that I control the construct of my mind because I visualize what I want, and I stay open to what and how it will show up. As I build within the fabric of my mind, I find my reality shows me where I am at. My narrative is that life is beautiful and magical, and we meet everyone for a reason and what we believe is very much what drifts into our view. This is very true.

Truth is to keep moving toward being awake and aware and authentic. It isn't all light, and it isn't all dark, but I will be real, raw, and ridiculous, and I will speak my truth to inspire, and I will be me.

Are you ready to do that? To be who you are? To be true and watch the view? Being real is power, especially in a world where most are hiding and afraid to speak the real raw truth of their experience.

As Terrence McKenna says, "Don't worry. You don't know enough to worry. Who do you think you are that you should worry" For cryin' out loud, it's a total waste of time. It presupposes such a knowledge of the situation that it is, in fact, a form of hubris."

I started to realize that we somehow seem to be great at constantly adding resistance to our journey because we have learned to—were taught to—doubt. That quiet faith we had as children fades as we get older. We have to reinstate and recommit our faith to ourselves and our journey at all costs. To leave people that don't believe in us, to make peace with the never-ending conflict we have within ourselves inside to bring our flow back to us. We must stop frantically searching around in the dark to keep picking up the dark pieces that keep weighing us down. We pick them up and put them down.

I think ninety-nine times, and I find nothing. I stop thinking, swim in the silence, and the truth comes to me. – Albert Einstein

It's hard to see the answers when fear is present. The only way to hear is to get quiet. To stop running around doing, to stop everything and sit in silence, and if you still can't hear because the noise is ever-present and won't let you be, try and just feel. If you feel excited about something, you are on the right path. If you feel lackluster about something, then it is not for you. Only you know. Only in the silence can you feel what you need to know. In the silence, your truth will always be waiting for you. Always. The universe and your intuition are sending you messages every single moment of the day about how you can heal, what's for you, and clues about what is next for you. Are you listening?

If you ignore it, you cannot heal it – Yung Pueblo

LAST THOUGHTS:

I want to leave you with these last thoughts, which came to me during an incredibly powerful trip I was on, in a time in my life where I was done with the bullshit stories about why I couldn't do something or show up for me. In a time where I finally stepped into my full power to show up and do all the things that excited me. In a time where I found myself happy exactly where I was as I surrendered to my truth and in a time where I only became available for my fuck yesses and let go of the fuck nos in my life.

What I am about to say is a simple concept, and yet in our humanness, we struggle with it, but the more we practice this and master it, we choose to give ourselves access to a lot more peace and happiness.

In a moment during one of my plant medicine trips and even outside of trips, I would have a feeling of energy rising. I would feel the way you do when you have too much caffeine and need to run around. You know the feeling when you're struggling with something heavy, and you struggle to sit still and be with it? It's a feeling of needing to move and or feeling like you want to jump out of your skin.

So I was feeling this and thinking it through and finding a way to surrender to it so it would most likely move through me. I wrote felt and heard this: I feel uncomfortable, often. I am unafraid now because I have been here so many times. I know this feeling, and I know it well. You've been here so many times, too, and you know it well. I am safe. You are safe. We are safe when we are uncomfortable.

I realized in this moment that I have never needed anything to change to be or feel safe. I have always been safe. In this moment, it was so clear. I felt such clarity about this as I surrendered into the feeling, and it moved through the view, and in an instant, it was gone. I realized then that we don't need anything to change or happen for us to feel safe in any moment because we are equipped in every moment to handle whatever it is. In our surrender and in our knowing that we are always safe, we dissolve everything. We will dissolve everything. We create, move, clear, and destroy in how we view and alchemize it through.

I hope you understand this, and if you already do, I hope you are able to embody it more and more each day because this is so powerful for your energy conservation and how you channel energy into creating the life you deserve and in loving yourself. You are in control of you.

I hope you live your best fucking life. Once you decide, you turn the tide, and everything will change for you. I believe in you. Please never give up and let no one and nothing stop you.

CPSIA information can be obtained
at www.ICGtesting.com
Printed in the USA
LVHW020733230421
685284LV00017B/946